THE HEART OF THE DEAL

the

HEART

of the

DEAL™

How to Invest and Negotiate
like a Real Estate Mogul

ANTHONY LOLLI
WITH BENJAMIN PLATT

DIVERSIONBOOKS

Diversion Books
A Division of Diversion Publishing Corp.
443 Park Avenue South, Suite 1008
New York, New York 10016
www.DiversionBooks.com

For more information, email info@diversionbooks.com

First Diversion Books edition June 2017.
Print ISBN: 978-1-68230-080-0
eBook ISBN: 978-1-68230-079-4

Contents

Introduction

First things first.

If you're looking for a way to get rich overnight, you may as well put this book down and go buy another. Then throw that book in the trash, because it's selling you a lie. I only know of two ways to get rich fast: win the lottery, or have a rich relative die and leave you their fortune. And if you need a book to tell you how to do either of those, you might have bigger problems to worry about.

If, however, you're interested in the unlimited earning potential of the real estate industry, and you're ready to put in the hard work to achieve your financial dreams, then this book is for you.

Real estate is a business where you get out of it what you put into it. You can turn it into passive income that can last you the rest of your life; you can do it as a part-time job. But those things come later. First, you have to put in the work. If you're ready and willing to do it, the rewards are out there waiting for you.

Let's Talk About Real Estate

I've been in the real estate business since I was nineteen years old. In that time, I've been an agent, a broker, a manager, a CEO, an investor, a landlord, and a consultant. I've rented apartments, I've bought and sold houses, I've renovated investment properties, and I've negotiated more deals than I can count. In other words, real estate has been at the center of every single day of my adult life.

Real estate is a unique industry. It revolves around one of humanity's most basic and essential needs—shelter—but unlike, for example, the food service industry, which also satisfies an essential need, you can look at any single real estate transaction and know that you're taking part in one of the most important moments of that person's life.

Simply in terms of price, a real estate transaction is one of the biggest purchases a person can make. And I'm not just talking about buying a house. Let's just look at what it takes to lease an apartment. These days in New York City, it's tough to find an apartment for less than $2,000 a month. Your typical lease will require the tenant to pay their first and last month's rent up front, as well as a one-month security deposit (if not more). So we're already up to $6,000. If there was a broker involved in the deal, you can add in a broker's fee, which is now often 15 percent of the annual rent—in this case $3,600. Add it all together, and you've got a total of nearly $10,000. That's not even including application fees, pet deposits, renter's insurance, or the very real possibility that the landlord could ask for more than one month's security.

Ten thousand dollars is a lot of money to drop in one sitting, and not something most people do every day. The only other common experience that compares is buying a car, and that's just if we're talking about renting an apartment. If we're talking about buying a house, then we could be looking at hundreds of thousands of dollars, plus taking on a mortgage, often the biggest and longest-lasting financial obligation of a person's life.

If the financial impact of a real estate transaction is huge, then what you get in return for that purchase is even bigger. I've had clients over the years who liked to say that they thought of their apartment as nothing more than four walls and a place to sleep, or as just a place to store their stuff. (And I've used those same arguments to convince clients to be realistic about their budget and take something they can afford, rather than holding out for an apartment like the ones they see on TV—it's a common salesman's refrain in cities where apartments are often tiny and expensive, but there's a lot to do just outside the door.)

But the truth is, whether it's an apartment or a house, it's much more than four walls and a bed. It's where you start and end your day. It's where you go to relax, where you go to get away from it all, where you go to be alone, and where you go to be with the people who mean the most to you. It's where you'll find comfort when you're sick, or sad, or just can't deal with the world. And it's also where you'll celebrate all kinds of firsts, triumphs, and personal milestones. In other words, it's home. Of all the millions of things you can possibly buy in this world, what's more important than that?

Helping someone find a home—whether as their real estate agent or as a landlord who welcomes them to your property—is an incredibly important, meaningful, and even intimate thing. You're helping them with one of the biggest decisions they'll ever face. That's why it's so important to approach working in this industry with the respect it deserves.

The real estate business gets a bad rap sometimes. At least according to pop culture and the court of popular opinion, the archetypal characters in real estate are the sleazy, backstabbing agent and the scummy, money-hungry landlord. I've met people who fit both of those descriptions. You can make a lot of money in real estate if all you care about is landing a fat commission or getting that rent check every month. But it's even more rewarding—both financially and personally—to keep the human element in mind.

Why? There's a whole laundry list of reasons, but number one is referrals.

One lesson that I teach everyone I work with is that the best kind of client you can ever have is one who's been referred to you by someone you've already worked with. Think about it: if people already think, even subconsciously, that real estate agents are all slimy and all landlords are interested in nothing but the monthly rent, then when you interact with a new client or tenant, you're already starting in a hole that you need to dig yourself out of in order to earn their trust. In other words, in order to prove that you're trustworthy, you first have to dispel the notion that you're not.

But with a referral client, they walk in the door already predisposed to like you. Think about the difference between someone who came to you because they happened to see your name on a website or at the bottom of some listing, versus someone who came to you because their friend told them: "He's an amazing agent. He did such a great job for me when I moved last year." Or: "There's an apartment opening up in my building. You should check it out. My landlord is so great."

It's a totally different scenario. With a referral client, it's much easier to establish trust, which means they'll be quicker to tell you what they really need in a home, which in turn means you'll be able to help them faster and more easily. And that adds up quicker closings, more closed deals, and more money in your pocket.

But make no mistake: real estate is a business, first and foremost. If you want to achieve financial independence, you'll have to be tough. You'll have to develop a thick skin. You'll have to be a fierce negotiator. But if you also keep in mind how important this is for the people you're working with, and how they're letting you into one of the biggest decisions of their lives, if you treat each deal with the respect it deserves, it will pay off for you time and time again. That's the Heart of the Deal.

PART 1

The Beginnings of a Businessman

Let's be honest: no kid ever says they want to be a broker when they grow up, and even fewer say they want to build a portfolio of investment properties. Despite the kind of lifestyle it can provide, no one starts out in life dreaming about real estate. And even among adults, real estate isn't for everyone. The hustle and grind, the feast or famine, the big risks for big rewards—it takes a certain type of person to forego the cushy comforts of a 9-to-5 and a steady paycheck to build their career around chasing commissions and investment returns.

Everyone who builds a career in real estate has their own unique path that got them there. In a way, my road to real estate actually did begin when I was a little kid. No, I wasn't running around the house in my dad's blazer, pretending to obtain imaginary listings. But the story of how I got to where I am today, the story of my rise from nothing to the founder of one of New York City's largest real estate firms, starts with a promise I made when I was just six years old. But to understand that, you first have to understand the two biggest influences on my life—my parents.

Mom and Dad

My mother, Gladys, immigrated to the United States from Ecuador with forty dollars to her name. She came here to get away from a bad marriage and to provide a better life for her son, my half-brother, whom she had to leave behind in Ecuador, hoping to send for him someday—only to find out later how hard it would be to get through all the red tape and get him out of the country. She spent her first few weeks in this country sleeping in an abandoned building with several other recent immigrants who, like her, had nowhere else to go. Her life in the States was difficult; the only work she could find was in a series of sweatshops. But eventually she made friends, found an apartment, and got work as a home attendant, then used the money she made to put herself through beauty school and become a beautician.

My father, Nicolas, was born to Italian immigrants. When he was seventeen, he lied about his age so he could enlist in the navy during World War II. After the war, he went to college on the GI Bill and ultimately became a New York public school teacher. He taught elementary school, high school, special ed—he even went to Riker's Island and taught the prisoners, often teaching them life skills like how to tie a tie or how to prepare for a job interview, on top of the academic knowledge he was there to impart. During the summers he sold insurance and taught music out of the back of his office to make a little extra money on the side.

The story of how these two people met, fell in love, and started a family together is the stuff movies are made of. But since you presumably picked up this book for business advice, and not for romance, I'll skip the sappy stuff and point out the obvious: these are two people who know a thing or two about hard work, and who never flinched from a challenge. They dreamed of a better life because they knew from experience what it meant to have a hard one, and they knew there was no sense sitting around all day

waiting for someone to hand them the life they wanted, because no one ever would.

When I was growing up, we lived in Brooklyn Heights—known even then to be one of the most affluent neighborhoods in the city—but while we walked by multimillion-dollar brownstones every day, my parents and I shared a one-bedroom shack. There were times when one or both of my parents would go hungry so that I would always have enough to eat. And yet, I always remember our home being full of warmth, full of family laughing and chatting away in English and Spanish. I never felt like anything was missing. Until one day I did.

When I was a young child, I'd ride the subway with my mother and she'd take me to the big department stores in Manhattan, like Barney's and Saks. My mother would try on fancy clothes and jewelry, but she would never buy anything. I didn't think anything was strange about it. At that age, kids think anything their parents do is just the normal way people act. Looking back now, it was obvious what was happening, but at the time it was just the fun way that my mother and I spent time together.

On one of these trips, I saw a waterproof watch on sale for eighteen dollars. I was instantly obsessed, the way that six-year-olds can get obsessed. It was the only thing in the world that mattered. I begged and pleaded with my mother to buy it for me, but she always made some excuse or found some way to distract me. This went on for weeks. Every time we went back, I'd see the watch and beg her to buy it for me. It got to the point where she would avoid that side of the store altogether, but even that only worked for so long. One day, when I asked her to buy me the watch, my mother simply ran out of excuses. She broke down in tears and admitted the real reason why she couldn't buy it for me—we couldn't afford it.

I was shocked. My parents worked so hard to provide for me, to make sure I always had everything I needed, that I just assumed we were rich. But when my mother told me that we couldn't afford

an eighteen-dollar watch, things suddenly clicked into place. At six years old, I was seeing things from a different perspective.

Just like that, it dawned on me that when I stayed over at other kids' houses, their families would always seem to have more than we had. They had more space. They had nicer furniture and decorations in their homes. They had a car, or even two cars, while we always took the train or the bus.

And that was when I understood why Mom loved to go to Saks, and admire all the clothes and jewelry and the perfumes. It was because she could afford to look—but that's all. It made me sad, and mad, when this sank in. I knew Mom deserved better than that.

Right then and there I made a promise to my mother: one day I would make our family rich so she could have all the nice things she deserved. I would buy her a big, white mansion for her to live in, and a big, white limousine to take her wherever she wanted to go.

Now, most parents, hearing their child make a pledge like that, would probably brush it off. But not my mother. She never let me forget it. Not for a day. And I can't thank her enough. Because, in time, I made good on that promise—white mansion and all. (Okay, she let me off the hook about the limo, but only because it was impractical. You try finding limo parking in Brooklyn!)

I didn't realize it at the time (did I mention I was six?), but I learned two incredibly valuable lessons that day:

1. **Always have a goal.** From that moment on, I had a dream that I was always working toward. I didn't have a plan, of course, but that would come later. But I had a goal—make my family rich; buy them a big, white mansion—and that would inspire me and keep me going through some of the most grueling, challenging days of my career.

2. **Always be as good as your word.** My mother could have ignored me. She could have just treated what I said as

the sweet but naïve certainty of a child and forgotten about it. But instead, she held me to it, because six years old or not, a promise is a promise.

All these years later, those two rules are just as important to me as they've ever been.

. . .

My father, Nicolas, taught me more than a few valuable lessons of his own. When I was a little older, he took a slightly early retirement from his many years of teaching when the city offered him what appeared to be a generous severance package. But when the money started coming in, it was a lot less than what he thought he'd be getting. This pension wasn't enough to feed his family, so he did what anyone would do—he started wandering the streets, convincing people to pay him to take their picture with a parrot.

Hmm…On second thought, maybe that's not what anyone would do.

Let me back up for a minute. The first time my father took my mother back to Ecuador to see her family, they visited the jungles of Puyo, where he was introduced to a captive blue-and-gold macaw. My father was so fascinated with the bird that he had it shipped back to New York. Followed by another. And another. At one point he had ten macaws in a New York apartment.

Macaws are beautiful, big, colorful birds. If you walk around with one, people are going to be drawn to you. And they're smart,

too. My father trained them to do all kinds of tricks, from whistling to lying down in people's arms like a baby, to memorizing a whole list of endearing phrases in English and Spanish, to blowing kisses.

So, when his pension wasn't enough to support his family, my father became the street entertainer known as the Bird Man. He'd walk around the popular areas of Manhattan with a macaw on his shoulder, sometimes until the middle of the night, and for a few bucks he'd put it on your arm, or your shoulder, or the top of your head, and snap your photo with the Polaroid camera he kept slung around his neck.

People absolutely loved him. Whether he was making the rounds between the nightclubs and restaurants of Little Italy or down at the South Street Seaport, wherever he went, he was a sensation. People would hire him for events, even high-profile functions with New York's elite. He was so beloved that, years later, when I was starting out in business, I had people who only worked with me or who gave me a special deal because I was the Bird Man's kid.

When I was old enough, my father would take me out with him some nights. That's how I got my first hands-on lessons in business. I'd go along with him and hand out cards to his customers with a list of answers to the most common questions he heard all the time (you can only hear "what kind of bird is that?" so many times before you start to plan ahead). Eventually he let me collect money and make change.

He taught me about the value of a dollar by taking me with him to buy film. He was always trying to save money, and sometimes he'd get burned in the effort. For example, he'd buy expired film—film that was past its sell-by date—at a discount, and maybe one out of ten pictures shot with that film would be no good. Sometimes the whole roll was bad, and he'd have wasted his money. I'd watch him buy film when he was broke and I got to see how he'd negotiate and get discounts.

He taught me the power of branding. He was always coming up with new ways to market himself. Those cards we handed out

didn't just have facts about the bird, they also had his contact info so people could hire him for events. He had a shirt made for me to wear when I went out with him that read PHOTO WITH THE PARROT. When he made enough money, he got a little three-wheel vehicle, like the ones cops use to give tickets today, and painted it to look like a macaw, and he decorated it with photos of celebrities getting their picture taken with one of his birds.

He taught me about the value of hard work. He'd be out there all night, pounding the pavement and cajoling tourists until he'd made enough money to take care of his family. By the time he came home, his feet were killing him, his back was killing him, and his clothes were covered in bird crap. And remember, this was supposed to be his retirement. The man was a veteran, he was a teacher for decades—these were supposed to be his golden years. But he went out there again and again, night after night, and I can't remember ever hearing him complain. Thanks to his dedication, we never had to worry about where our next meal would come from or whether we'd have a roof over our heads.

But the biggest lesson he taught me was the power of charm.

Let's do an exercise. Picture a swanky Manhattan restaurant, a real hotspot where the elite come to see and be seen. Imagine walking into a place like that and telling the maître d' that you have no intention of buying anything and, in fact, you would like his permission to walk around the restaurant, asking the customers for money. And imagine you're doing all this with a huge bird on your shoulder and a line of fresh bird shit on the back of your jacket.

Who do you think they'd call first—the health inspector or the police?

But when my father did it, the response was, "Of course! Come on in!" That's charm. When a woman would shriek and recoil when she noticed the bird on his shoulder because she was terrified of animals, and within seconds he had her cooing with delight with the bird in her arms—that's charm. When influential politicians would let the bird crawl all over them at a public event, grinning like a kid the whole time, not caring what they looked like in front of all the cameras—that's charm. And when things were tight and he had to convince shop owners to act against their own self-interest and give him film for free, just so he could get back out there and try to make a few bucks—you'd better believe that's charm.

My father taught me a lot of valuable lessons, but none of them were more important, or left a bigger impression, than the power of personality. He taught me that no matter what you're selling, you're selling yourself first.

I Get in the Game

How I learned what I wanted, got my real estate
license, and ended up working for myself

I didn't get into real estate right away. First I went through a series of odd jobs that taught me more about what I didn't want from a career than anything else. If it sounds like I'm knocking these

experiences, I'm not. Sometimes learning what you don't want is a crucial step in figuring out what you do want.

I was a bike messenger, where I learned, well...mostly that I didn't want to be a bike messenger. And even if I did, that particular job path was cut off for me when I was in a nasty car accident that injured my spine. I actually had to finish my high school education from home, but thanks to the support of my parents and a particularly wonderful teacher who took the time to work with me one-on-one, I still graduated on time.

Later, I sold eyeglasses at a store off Madison Avenue. It was my first experience working in a professional environment, and it showed. I remember on my first day I asked my manager how to do something by starting with, "Yo, how do you...?" He taught me what I wanted to know, but the first thing he told me? "Don't call me Yo." Working there taught me about corporate discipline, about how to balance work and friendship, and about how to act in a proper professional manner, but it wasn't for me. I learned that I wasn't meant for a typical 9-to-5, and that's important. I don't care if you've dreamed of being an entrepreneur since you were in diapers—if you've never worked in a traditional work environment, you'll never have the foundation for thriving in a nontraditional one.

Being stuck inside the same four walls every day wasn't for me. No problem. Next I went to work with my cousin Victor, installing security systems. On paper, this was a great opportunity for me. The work took us to different places every day. I got to work on some pretty impressive homes—including properties owned by big-time celebrities like Bruce Springsteen and Jon Bon Jovi—as well as some of New York's most prestigious commercial buildings. I got to meet all kinds of different people. The money was nothing to sneeze at. I even got to work with family—and Victor was a great boss; he really went out of his way to take me under his wing. In theory, it should have all worked out perfectly. In reality...let's just say there's a reason this isn't a book about getting rich through security system installation.

I was a terrible employee and I knew it. My heart just wasn't in it. I was so bad that when the time came for Victor to give me my first paycheck, I told him not to bother, I wasn't going to cash it. My cousin didn't have the heart to fire a member of his own family—which speaks volumes about what a great guy he was, and still is—so I saved him the trouble by quitting.

That experience taught me that I wouldn't be happy doing something I wasn't passionate about. It may sound obvious, but that's actually a critical lesson to learn about yourself. There are a lot of people in this world who are perfectly content doing a job they don't really care about, so long as it's not too unpleasant and the pay is good enough for their needs. Well, here the pay was perfectly good for my age, with room to grow, and there wasn't really anything about the job I actively disliked. But I was never going to be passionate about installing security systems, and because of that, I couldn't commit to it fully. And without commitment, you're destined to fail.

All these jobs also taught me that I would never really be happy working for someone else. I needed a job that would let me work on my own terms. In short, I was destined to be an entrepreneur; I just didn't know it yet.

My first foray into real estate actually came a few years earlier, well before I ever got my salesperson's license. My father had saved up and purchased a run-down multiunit rental property in Brooklyn's Park Slope neighborhood. Today Park Slope is one of the most expensive and sought-after neighborhoods in NYC, but at the time it was just the opposite—a deeply troubled, crime-ridden area that people avoided as much as they could. The building was a block from the projects, and break-ins were a constant problem. My father did everything he could to fix up the building and make it safer and more appealing, but he still had difficulty finding tenants for the property. He had purchased the building for very little money down, so if he didn't start making money from it quickly, the mortgage payments would eat him alive.

Tenant after tenant paid the rent late or didn't pay at all. When he tried evicting some, they reacted with violence and I can recall

a time when they came with a hammer and were banging on our apartment door, trying to get in—to go after my father.

This first experience as a landlord left a bad taste in his mouth. He got to the point where he didn't want anything to do with real estate. This house was the only building he ever purchased and despite the rocky start, things took a turn when a family friend suggested that he rent it to the young Jehovah's Witnesses who came to Brooklyn to work at Bethel, their organization's headquarters.

My father took that advice. I was raised as a Jehovah's Witness, so we had ties to that community, and my father was able to spread the word about his vacant apartments. He began renting out the units to young Jehovah's Witnesses for forty dollars a night. By appealing to a niche market, he was suddenly had every apartment filled, night after night.

I was about sixteen at the time, and I got involved by helping my father manage the property, mostly just collecting rent payments and making sure the apartments were in good shape between one tenant and the next.

Then it occurred to me—these were big apartments we were renting out, but the people staying there were really only treating them like hotel rooms—i.e., as a place to sleep, rather than a place to live. It made sense; they wanted to stay in Brooklyn to be close to work, but at the time there weren't many hotels in Brooklyn, and staying in Manhattan would have been prohibitively expensive for them. They weren't moving in—in the sense of filling these apartments with their own furniture and belongings—or having parties there. They had come to Brooklyn to work at Bethel, and that was really the center of their lives. Given that, I realized that we could increase our earnings by dividing up the apartments into separate rooms, so we could rent out each one individually. We gave it a shot, charging forty dollars per room instead of per apartment. In a sense, we were turning our apartment building into an early version of Airbnb. And just like that, our income shot up.

I was still a teenager, and suddenly I was managing a hotel, of sorts. Running a hotel, of course, is very different from running an

apartment building, because of the high turnover and the need for daily maintenance. It was challenging work, but I saw a demand for more of this sort of enterprise in Brooklyn. Although it would still be several years before Brooklyn became the hot destination that it is today, I could already sense a change starting to build, and I knew the demand for short-term accommodations in the borough was only going to go up.

With the success of this first minihotel, I thought we could replicate this model all over Brooklyn—buying old apartment buildings on the cheap, whipping them into shape, and splitting the units up into individual rooms to rent out by the night. Maybe we could even make them bed-and-breakfasts, adding in the extra appeal of a home-cooked meal. This felt like an idea that could generate the kind of money I was looking for—buy your parents a big, white mansion money.

I started putting together a plan of attack. I even footed the bill for a family friend to go through a respected hospitality management program so she could help with the business. But ultimately, while I was right about the winds of change sweeping through Brooklyn, at my age, and with the limited resources available to me at the time, there was no way I could get in front of it.

Luxury apartment buildings were already on the rise in Brooklyn, including in Park Slope. Young professionals who were priced out of Manhattan were moving to Brooklyn in slow, but steadily increasing numbers. And where there's new money flowing into a neighborhood, restaurants and retail are always right behind. And where there's restaurants and retail, there are hotels. The death knell of my plan came when I heard that Marriott was going to be breaking ground on a giant hotel in Brooklyn. If the hospitality giants already had their eye on the borough, I was too late.

• • •

At nineteen, I was still trying to figure out what I wanted to do, what path to go down next. That's when I ran into the father of an old friend of mine. As long as I'd known them, their family had been pretty poor, just like mine. And yet, my friend's dad was driving a nice, new car and wearing better clothes than I'd ever seen on him. He looked like a new man.

I asked him what he'd been up to, and he explained that he had recently gotten his real estate salesperson's license, and had started making money right away. Well, I thought to myself, if he could do it, I could do it. All my life I'd walked by those million-dollar brownstones, like giant reminders of everything my family didn't have, perched right outside our doorstep. In just a few weeks, I was going to be buying and selling those things.

I immediately enrolled in a licensing course at a Brooklyn real estate school. Through the classes, the instructor constantly talked about how much money there was to be made in real estate. As much as I liked the sound of that, something didn't sit right with me. This guy clearly knew the real estate business—he was teaching a class on it, after all—so if real estate was so lucrative, why wasn't he out there doing it himself, instead of being stuck in this classroom? Why wasn't he putting his money where his mouth was? One day, during class, I asked him just that. The other students snickered, but not the instructor. He just smiled and told me to stick around after class, and he'd explain. I did, and it turned out that his secret was pretty simple: "I don't just teach at this school," he said. "I own the school."

Suddenly it clicked into place. This guy was teaching us to become agents, about making sales, but the real estate industry was about more than agents and brokers. It was about investors and landlords, architects and developers, mortgage brokers and attorneys, even teachers. I knew all of this, of course, but it was only in that moment that the scale of the industry—all the different entry points into the business—really hit home. I had wondered why the teacher wasn't putting his money where his mouth was, but it turned out that's exactly what he was doing. Only instead of doing it through sales, he was doing it through investment and education. I did the math in my head, multiplying the cost each

student paid to take the course by the number of students in the course at once, and multiplied that by the number of courses he taught each year. At $175 per student for a one-week course, this guy was easily clearing over $1 million a year.

Needless to say, I was convinced.

I was fired up. I decided that I wanted to follow in this guy's footsteps. I would start off by selling properties, then use the profits to start my own real estate company where I'd buy buildings. Then I'd start my own construction company to fix them up. And then, I'd open a real estate school in one of my buildings so I could bring all my friends and family into the business too.

I would have opened my own company the second I got my real estate license if I could. Unfortunately, that's not the way it works. In order to start your own real estate firm, you need a broker's license, and in New York, to get a broker's license, you first need to spend at least two years working at someone else's brokerage.

So, step one: I needed someone to hire me.

With my real estate salesperson's license in hand, I went to my friend's father, and he got me a meeting with the owner of the firm where he was working in Brooklyn Heights. The owner was a nice guy, very forthcoming and informative. He took me around the office, walked me around the neighborhood, and showed me some of his properties. He spent most of the afternoon with me, in fact, and I was getting my hopes up. I thought I was hired, and that I'd be out there the next morning making deals and conquering the world. But then he sat me down in a café and told me, "You know, kid, I'd like to hire you, but I can't. You're way too young. This is an older neighborhood; the people are used to older brokers. You'll make it in real estate, if you want to—just not in this neighborhood."

So I applied to other brokerages. I went right to the top, to the most famous firms in town. The first one I spoke to said I was too young. So did the next one. And the next. Finally, though, one of the biggest firms in Brooklyn took a chance on me.

The company itself may have been willing to overlook my age, but that didn't mean the other agents in the office felt the same way. They didn't want some kid hanging around. I'd come into the office and find all the other agents' coats piled on my desk and chair. Or they'd disconnect my desk phone, which may not sound like that big of a deal now, but this was back when not everyone had a cell phone, and if you wanted to reach a real estate agent, you still called their office line. That meant that all the clients who were trying to reach me were getting a disconnected signal, getting frustrated, and trying someone else at the company. In other words: they were stealing my leads.

There was one agent at the company who didn't treat me like dirt, and who actually let me shadow him when I was first starting out. This guy was bringing in deals left and right. And he was totally blind. If this guy could sell houses without even being able to see what they looked like, what excuse did I have for not giving it my all? Somehow, "people whose respect I haven't earned are being mean to me" didn't feel like a valid reason for giving up anymore.

Fortunately, I had an ace up my sleeve to help me get started. Reputation means a lot in real estate, and when you're first starting out, you typically don't have one. But while no one knew me as Anthony Lolli, the Real Estate Agent, there were still plenty of people who knew me as Anthony Lolli, the Son of the Bird Man. And that little bit of branding went a long way in those early days of my career. I was able to secure listings because the owners remembered my father's act, and they remembered me following him around when I was younger. I even got a few listings in Brooklyn Heights, although most of the business the company had me doing was at the lower end of the spectrum.

Right from the start, I threw myself into being an agent. Within my first year I was one of the highest-producing agents at the firm in terms of volume. How did I make that happen? Having a personal brand courtesy of my father helped at the beginning, for sure, but the real reason is this: I got it because I went after it.

I'll share one of the Essential Truths of the Universe with you right now: there is no substitute for hard work. You have to go hard

until hard isn't hard anymore. And that's exactly what I did. I got up early, I went to bed late, if I went to bed at all. I went after the business at every possible opportunity.

A lot of new agents, when they're first starting out, will see someone sticking up a FOR SALE BY OWNER sign on their property, and they'll just drive on by. They tell themselves, "they don't want to work with someone so inexperienced. If they wanted an agent, they'd get an agent. There's no way I could convince them to work with me." They forget that you'll never get the experience unless you put yourself out there. They're not just setting themselves up to fail; they've already failed because they didn't give themselves the chance to succeed.

Now, me, when I saw someone putting up a sign like that, I was out of my car so fast it was a 50/50 shot whether I'd even remember to park it first. I forced myself to do it at first—I didn't let myself off the hook or swear I'd do it the next time—until I didn't have to force myself anymore, because it had become a habit. And yes, I got rejections. Half of surviving in real estate is dealing with rejections. But I also got a lot of business that way. And a couple years later, that habit would be the key to one of the most important days of my career.

I started dominating my market, and securing exclusive listings on some million-dollar houses and condos, as well as some of Brooklyn's first wave of luxury apartments. But the company still had me doing the majority of my work in lower-end neighborhoods. Between that and the way their commissions were structured, I wasn't making as much money as I thought I was worth, particularly since I'd proven myself as an agent. Despite all that I'd accomplished over that first year, the company still wasn't going to set me up with territory in Brooklyn Heights, like I wanted. That was still the brass ring for me. So, I decided to leave my firm, believing that my track record from that first year would be enough to get me in the door of a high-end Brooklyn Heights firm. It was risky to leave one job before I'd lined up the

next one, but I was cocky. And besides, if you don't gamble on yourself, who will?

As it turned out, I might have jumped the gun a little. I applied to fourteen different brokerages in Brooklyn Heights, and every single one of them slammed the door in my face. To them, it didn't matter how many deals I'd closed in my first year on the job, or how much promise I had. I was still too young and too rough around the edges in their eyes; they thought no one would trust someone like me to sell their $3 million townhouse.

After I'd been out of work for a few days, I was getting pretty nervous, and starting to think that maybe I'd been hasty jumping ship before I'd lined up another job. One day, as I was canvassing Brooklyn Heights as usual—just scouting around, hoping for something to turn up—I noticed a sign on an old brownstone building that pointed me to a real estate office on the second floor. It was a raggedy, dusty office, with just one old, stooped, defeated-looking broker hunched over a desk covered in papers. When I told him that I was looking for a company to latch onto he said, "Sorry, kid. I can't help you. I'm not hiring. I can't afford to, and I wouldn't have the time to train you if I did. And anyway, I'm getting sued by my former partners. I spend all my time dealing with lawsuits. I haven't done any actual real estate brokerage in years."

Maybe if I'd been a little older, I would have just walked away. I mean, when someone tells you they're being sued by their ex–business partners, it doesn't exactly paint a great picture. But this guy had open office space smack in the middle of Brooklyn Heights, and I wanted it. Bad.

Part of being a successful salesman is recognizing when an objection can be overcome. If someone says they need three bedrooms and the apartment you're showing only has one, well, there's not a lot you can do about that (and honestly, why were you showing it to them in the first place?). But if someone says they can't stand the paint color, that's an easy fix. (I'll go over how to overcome objections that are a lot stronger than paint color later on.)

In this case, I had fourteen different offices tell me I was too young. There wasn't anything I could do about that; I couldn't make myself older just by wanting it. But this guy's excuse for not giving me a job was that he didn't think he could afford it, and that he didn't have the time to train me. Well, I wasn't looking for someone to train me, and as for payment, with the money I was sure I could make working in Brooklyn Heights, I knew I could work out an arrangement that would benefit both of us. I told him about myself and what I was looking for. In the end, he agreed to take me on as an agent, but only if I split everything with him 50/50—the commissions and the bills. It was a crazy arrangement, and I knew it, but I also knew that this guy could be my only chance at setting up shop in Brooklyn Heights. We had a deal. True to his word, the broker gave me no training whatsoever, or really any kind of support beyond the use of his office space. But he gave me a chance, and that was all I needed.

Once I got going, it turned out my age wasn't a problem at all. I knew the neighborhood like the back of my hand, I knew how to sell, and I knew the importance of working hard every single day. That was all I needed. Over the next year, I put all the lessons I'd learned at my old company to work: I pounded the pavement, I spent every day showing properties and every evening forming relationships with local sellers and property managers, I worked seven days a week, and ultimately I built myself into one of the highest-producing agents in Brooklyn Heights. I even hired a team of nine agents to work with me. Like me, most of my agents grew up poor in an affluent neighborhood, and were ready to hustle day in and day out to get a piece of that high life for themselves and their families. I taught them the ropes myself, and soon we were a well-oiled machine.

It wasn't long before the brokers who had turned me down for a job were knocking down my door to try to get me to come work for them. I was being courted by so many different firms that there was a period of about six months when I don't think I paid for a single meal. But even at that age, I put a high premium on loyalty. Even though the office I was working out of wasn't glamorous, even though the commission split wasn't generous and I had to shoulder half the office's expenses, I turned down every offer that came my way. I wanted to stick by the broker who took a chance on me.

Unfortunately, my loyalty was not returned in kind. After a while, my broker's legal and financial troubles must have gotten the better of him, because he stopped paying the team of agents I'd brought on board. One by one, they left the company. Who could blame them? And once there was no one else left at the company for him to screw over, it was my turn.

Looking back, I don't know why I stuck around as long as I did. I knew he'd had serious problems with his business partners before, I saw how he withheld payments from the other agents. But I'd basically saved his company. I was bringing in deals left and right. If there was one person I thought he'd go to the ends of the earth to keep around, I thought it was me. And then he stiffed me on thirty thousand dollars' worth of commissions. What choice did I have? I had to walk.

Unlike the last time I left a job, though, this time I had lucrative prospects available to me. I had serious offers on the table from some of Brooklyn's real estate titans, with much better splits than I had been getting before. All I had to do was decide which one to accept, and soon that missing $30,000 would be a distant memory.

That's when my mother asked me a good question: "Why do you want to work so hard to build up someone else's company and risk having the same thing happen all over again, when you could start your own?"

She was right. At that point, I'd worked as a salesperson long enough that I could qualify for a broker's license and open my own office, even though I was only twenty-one. And even if I went to work for the most reputable firm in the city, there was no guarantee that I wouldn't end up getting screwed over (in fact, the offer I was most seriously considering came from a company that ended up closing down its operations in Brooklyn just a few years later).

It's not like I was the first person in the history of real estate to be robbed of a commission. It could happen anywhere.

But now I had experience, I had a reputation, I had the know-how. It would be a risk—it would mean eating into the savings I'd been building up to fulfill the promise I'd made to my mother when I was six, and it would mean losing out on who know how many deals' worth of commission while I set up shop. But the chance to be my own boss, to have my own firm, the potential for future earnings…it turned out the choice was really no choice at all.

The Rise of Rapid Realty

How I started a company, started a portfolio, and started to change the game

As soon as I made the decision to open my own firm, I was energized like never before, and I couldn't wait to get started.

Step 1: Find an office space. The first thing was to start looking for an office space to rent in—where else?—Brooklyn Heights. It was where I'd always wanted to work, it was where I'd spent the last year building a reputation, and it was only one subway stop from Manhattan, making it an easy stepping stone to doing real estate in the city.

Once I set my mind on something, it's all I think about. It's the only thing I want to do. So it's safe to say that I would have looked at every last commercial space in the neighborhood to find the perfect one if my mother hadn't stepped in to be the voice of reason once again. "Why do you want to rent a place in Brooklyn Heights?" she said. "When you pay rent, you're just throwing your money away. *Poof*, it's gone. For what you'd pay to rent a space there, you could buy a building just a little bit further into Brooklyn. At least that way you might be able to make some

money on it." I didn't know it, but that piece of advice was about to change my life.

Sometimes things have a way of lining up just right. For me, this was one of those times. Just after I'd had that conversation with my mother, I was driving home down 4th Avenue in the south part of Park Slope when I saw a man sticking a FOR SALE sign up in front of a three-story, mixed-use building. At that time, this part of Park Slope was still in pretty rough shape. The building was a block away from a methadone clinic, and there were addicts everywhere you looked, some passed out on the sidewalk, some just wandering in a daze.

You know how I said that as an agent, you have to train yourself to go after any listing you see? Well, my training was in full effect that day, because before the thought even crossed my mind that this could be a potential place for me to open my business, I had pulled over, parked (let's just call it semilegally), and leapt out of the car to go try to get that listing.

Remember, at this point I had just quit my job and I hadn't actually started my company yet. If I got the listing, I wouldn't be able to do anything but sit on it until I got myself set up. But that wasn't about to stop me. Like I said, training in action.

As it turned out, the man was a priest and the building was owned by the church. He gave me a tour of the property and I walked out with an exclusive right-to-sell agreement. After giving it some thought, though, I realized that, despite the unsafe feel of the surrounding area, this building could actually be the perfect spot for me to set up my new company. It was right at the top of what I could afford, but it was doable, and it was located on one of Brooklyn's most heavily trafficked streets, meaning it would get good exposure from people driving by every day. While the neighborhood was still rough, there was no doubt in my mind that it was going to improve and property values would rise as people got priced out of the trendier northern end of Park Slope, and because it was a mixed-use building, I could set up my office on the

ground floor and rent out the upper-floor apartments to generate some passive income to support my new business.

The location of the building got me thinking about the core concept of the entire business I was about to launch. I had originally wanted to set up shop in Brooklyn Heights and use that as a stepping stone to Manhattan. But, as I knew from experience, Brooklyn Heights already had a lot of well-established brokerages, and even those were a drop in the bucket compared to how crowded the Manhattan market was. This building was located further into Brooklyn, though, making a quick transition into Manhattan real estate that much more difficult. So why focus on Manhattan at all? Brooklyn was bigger, it was primed for growth, and it was where I'd spent my entire life, so I knew it like my own face.

And the more I thought about Brooklyn and its needs, the more I thought about rentals. At that time, everyone wanted to be working in sales. Everyone knew that's where the big money was. But if everyone already knew it, how much money would there really be for a new guy like me? In sales, I'd be fighting for a tiny piece of the pie, and I'd be fighting against companies that had been doing it for a lot longer and had a lot more muscle to throw around. But rentals? Practically no one was paying any attention to rentals, especially in the outer boroughs. Rentals were something most New York real estate companies did to pad their earnings between sales, if they did them at all. And even then, they only worked on the most expensive luxury buildings. Renters below the very top end of the spectrum were generally left to track down vacancies and contact management companies all on their own if they wanted to apply for an apartment.

So, I had a choice. I could fight every other real estate company in New York, some that had been in business for over a century, and be a very tiny fish in a very big pond, or I could focus on the underserved rental market and pretty much have the pond to myself.

Going the sales route would be easier. The road map was already laid out for me. It might mean dealing with a huge number of competitors, but it would also mean having a huge number of successful examples to follow. Rentals were riskier. What if there was a good reason that no one else was putting rentals first? The commissions from each deal would be much smaller, meaning I'd need to maintain a much higher volume. And there would be no path laid out for me to follow.

The more I thought about it, the more rentals called to me. It wouldn't be easy, but it's like they say: pigeons flock together, eagles fly alone. And New York already had enough pigeons. My mind was made up. And with that decision, Rapid Realty NYC was born.

Step 2: Renovations. The building had a lot of potential, but it was in rough shape. It needed some serious renovations. The only problem was, because I'd maxed out my budget buying the building in the first place, I didn't have enough money left over to pay for professional contractors. So I did the only thing I could: I hired day laborers and I rolled up my sleeves and worked right alongside them. Every morning I'd round up a crew of laborers, spend the day working on the renovations, and then I'd go out into the neighborhood in the evenings to try to meet local landlords and acquire some listings to get my business off the ground.

They say that adversity is the best teacher, and in this case that definitely proved to be true. If I could have hired contractors, I probably would have let them handle the whole renovation wall-to-wall. But working with the day laborers gave me a hands-on education in construction that would have taken years of property management to equal, knowledge that has served me well in every building I've ever bought, in the design and construction

of my own home, and even in the construction of future Rapid Realty franchises.

In 1998, Rapid Realty officially opened for business.

We started out with three agents, all friends of mine. I helped them get their licenses and spent the day training them while continuing to go out and hunt for listings in the evenings. We did all our work on a single computer that we shared on the ground floor of the building. Renting out the apartments upstairs was the top priority, and once we'd gotten that squared away, the rental income helped to cover the bills while I got the whole operation whirring up to speed.

As I'd already learned, getting people to trust you with their real estate transactions when you're young can be difficult, but it helps if you have the brand power of a reputable firm behind you. That gives you instant respectability. When you're young and working for a company no one's ever heard of because it's only existed for a week? That's a tough sell. I was only twenty-one at this point, just two years older than when I'd gotten my license. No one knew what Rapid Realty was. Every listing we got was a challenge; every deal we closed was a victory.

Fortunately, by that point, I was very accustomed to having to convince people to look past my age and take a chance on me, and I was able to teach my small team of agents to do the same. The fact that we were specializing in rentals turned out to be a double-edged sword. Landlords in that area weren't used to some unknown broker knocking on their door claiming to want to help them rent their vacant units. We had to deal with a fair amount of suspicion from people who figured we had to have some kind of crooked angle. But on the other hand, the stakes weren't as high as they would be if we were trying to get people to let us sell their homes for them, so landlords were willing to take a chance on us. The fact that I owned a property in the neighborhood definitely helped—it showed that I was invested in the area (literally) and that I understood a landlord's mentality.

Bit by bit, deal by deal, we started to prove ourselves, finding

tenants for landlords faster than they had ever done on their own. Within a year, I'd made enough money renting apartments that I was able to buy another multiunit building in Downtown Brooklyn.

Unlike my first property, this one was fully occupied when I bought it. In order to realize a good rate of return on my investment, I knew I would need to renovate the entire building in order to command higher rents on the apartments. I was faced with the choice that every property investor encounters before long: do I wait for the current leases to expire, or do I take on the additional expense, to say nothing of the awkwardness and potential unpleasantness, of trying to buy out each of the tenants?

In this case, the choice was really no choice at all. The units in the building were renting for well below market rate for the area, which was why I was able to get a good deal on the building itself. But if I couldn't renovate and charge a fair rate, I may as well have thrown that money in the trash. So, although I was a little nervous about it, I successfully negotiated buyouts with each of the tenants in the building and started renovations right away. (I'd go on to negotiate hundreds of buyouts, both for my own properties and on behalf of other investors who needed help working with stubborn tenants. Later in this book, I'll share some of my biggest buyout successes, plus a couple of horror stories!)

Soon I had my second investment property fully renovated, using the construction lessons I'd learned from working on my first. And with the growing strength of Rapid Realty behind me, the building was fully rented as soon as it was ready. My company was picking up steam. I was already imagining what that white mansion would look like.

And then, it all went horribly wrong.

Just three months after the renovations had been completed on my new property, one of my tenants, a young woman, fell into a diabetic coma while she had several aromatherapy candles burning. The firefighters later told me that her bedsheets had caught fire. The flames spread throughout the whole building. By some miracle, the building was mostly empty at that time and no one else was hurt, but the young woman died of smoke inhalation.

That moment hit me like a runaway subway train. Everything came to a screeching halt. I was still in my early twenties, still just a kid, and the sheer enormity of it…When something like that happens, you can't help but torture yourself wondering if it was somehow your fault, if there was anything you could have done. Was everything up to code, like I thought? Was there any way I could have made it safer? What if someone else had been home? On and on.

That's the thing about real estate. The good days are so good. You give someone a place to live, you take care of that basic necessity and give them a place where they can feel comfortable and secure, and you make good money doing it. That's a great feeling on every level, and there are a lot of days like that. But all these years later I still have a hard time thinking about the bad days.

The woman's tragic death was hard enough. But adding to the tragedy, the fire left the building completely uninhabitable. Buying and renovating the building had taken every cent I had, and now I somehow needed to rebuild and I didn't even have the passive income from the property itself to help me do it. I felt like I was at a crossroads. I thought about the years I'd already put into learning this business, the doors that had been slammed in my face, and how hard I'd worked to prove myself. I thought about the blood and sweat I'd put into opening Rapid Realty and getting it off the ground, and how proud my parents were when it had started to do well. I thought about the agents who were looking to me every day to show them the ropes, who had put their faith in me to help them build their careers.

I went back to work, and I went harder than ever. I spent seven days a week renting apartments, and in the evenings I used my construction knowledge and connections to find work as a general contractor. I didn't let up for a second. And it paid off. Over the next few years, Rapid Realty slowly grew, and so did my portfolio of rental properties.

Over that time, Brooklyn was undergoing a startling transformation of its own. Even before I started Rapid Realty, I had felt like Brooklyn was on the cusp of something amazing. As late as 2000, it wasn't uncommon for taxis to refuse to go to Brooklyn. But within a few short years, all that changed, as people flocked to Brooklyn in record-breaking numbers and the rise of Brooklyn as a brand unto itself became a global phenomenon, making the borough a hot destination for both residents and tourists.

There are a lot of factors that all came together to create such a drastic change in Brooklyn in such a short span of time. For instance, increasingly exorbitant prices in Manhattan had been driving renters across the bridge in steadily increasing numbers for a while. Artists who envisioned themselves living in airy lofts in Soho found that they couldn't actually do it without leading a secret double life as an investment banker. But over in Brooklyn, that kind of lifestyle was still available on the cheap (relatively). And wherever the artists go, they are soon followed by the yuppies who like the idea of living near the artists. And where there are yuppies, there's retail, and retail attracts the families. It's a story as old as cities. But if I had to point to one specific moment that shifted the attention of the real estate market from Manhattan to Brooklyn, it would be another tragedy—9/11.

There's no doubt in my mind that Brooklyn would have become a hot destination on its own, eventually. But there's also no doubt that September Eleventh accelerated the process. It feels ghoulish to look at the worst terrorist attack in American history and say that it helped my business. But the fact is, as someone who was in New York on that horrible day, and who was working in the real estate industry, to me it seemed like when the towers came down, everyone who had been hunting for an apartment in Manhattan suddenly took a breath, looked around, considered their options, and decided to move to Brooklyn instead.

Practically overnight, the demand for housing in Brooklyn shot through the roof. (Don't get me wrong, there was still plenty of demand for Manhattan. I mean, it's Manhattan. You could hop

in a time machine and go a thousand years into the future, and people would still be fighting over three-hundred-square-foot studios.) But what I noticed was that it happened so quickly and so suddenly that a lot of landlords didn't know how to deal with it.

A lot of these landlords came from families that had owned these properties for generations, and who had always rented them out to people who lived and worked in that specific neighborhood, and had likely grown up around the block. Many of them weren't used to renting to students, for instance, and had never worked with a guarantor or looked at application paperwork from someone who lived out of state. Others had never established a policy about having pets in the apartment simply because it had never come up.

Or you had ethnic enclaves, like the Polish enclave up in Greenpoint, where owners had been renting out apartments for decades without ever needing to speak a word of English, who were now dealing with inquiries from prospective renters who didn't speak any Polish and only wanted the apartment because it was close to their favorite underground concert venue. And let me tell you, old-school Brooklyn people are resistant to change, and get suspicious when strangers come knocking.

My team and I occupied a unique space at that point because we were young—we understood what all these new people flocking to Brooklyn were looking for—but we also understood the more traditional ways that the local landlords were accustomed to operating. And because we were all from Brooklyn, we'd all grown up there, we had trust from both sides. Sometimes I felt like my job was translating Hipster into Landlord and back. There were times when I had to sit down with a landlord whose approach to renting apartments had always been, "Eh, stick the rent under my door on the first of the month and you can do what you want," and teach them how to read a credit report.

So, there was a learning curve. Once landlords began to realize how much more money they could get for their apartments if they just adapted to the demands of the market, they came around in a hurry. In Park Slope South, especially, I tried to lead by example with my own steadily growing portfolio of properties, which I was now renovating with my own construction crew. With each renovation, I tried to attract renters at a higher price point by adding in luxury touches, like high-end finishes, while retaining the Brooklyn charm they wanted by keeping elements like exposed brick walls. Soon, other landlords in the area were coming to me to ask me to consult on their next renovation, or even to help them with negotiating tenant buyouts on recently acquired properties so they could renovate in the first place.

During this time, Rapid Realty also led the charge in introducing local landlords to the idea of no-fee apartments. "No-fee" is actually a bit of a misnomer—you'd be amazed by how many people think it means that the broker doesn't receive any kind of compensation at all. What it actually means is that there's no broker fee for the tenant; the landlord pays the broker fee instead. In a high-demand market, landlords who choose to list their apartments as no-fee can often stand out and attract tenants faster than a similar property across the street that wants the tenants to pay the broker fee, even if the rent at the place across the street is actually a little cheaper.

So, business was booming. By the age of twenty-three, I'd become a millionaire. I still remember the first thing I bought when I realized I'd reached that level of success: a Rolex Masterspiece with the Presidential band, which had three shades of gold—yellow, rose, and white. It had a meteorite dial, a diamond bezel, and cost me $36,000. I bought a Rolex for my mother, too. They might not have been waterproof, but they were a symbol of that moment when I was six years old that set me on this path. I was acquiring at least one new rental property each year and renovating them with my own crew. Rapid Realty grew to fifteen agents. I even hired a secretary.

I realize it sounds a little strange to end the story of how I triumphantly recovered from a crushing tragedy, led the charge to capitalize on a sudden market shift, and became a millionaire with, "I hired a secretary," but it was a big deal for me. Up to that point,

Rapid Realty was a company of agents. It was me and my team, and we all did one thing—rent apartments. Any administrative stuff that needed doing, I just did it myself. But now we'd grown to the point where doing it all myself wasn't an option. I had to hand some of the day-to-day administrative stuff off to someone else. In other words, the company was now big enough to need support staff. Handing off any responsibility for the operations of the company I'd started, even if it was just answering phones and filing paperwork, was very hard for me, but it was a necessary change. That, for me, is the moment when I stopped just being the boss and became a CEO.

Before long, I was making enough money that I was able to start taking care of my parents, and they were both able to retire (for real this time). But just because they didn't have to work anymore didn't mean they didn't still want to. Neither of my parents was ever the type to just sit idle all day. So I renovated the floor above the Rapid Realty office, turning it from apartments into a real estate school. Opening a real estate school had been part of my vision ever since that day I stayed after class to talk to my teacher.

But in honor of my father's lifelong commitment to education, I gave the school to my parents as a gift. Under their ownership, that school would go on to give tens of thousands of people their introduction to the world of real estate.

The school ended up being a perfect fit for my father. I had tried to find ways to get him involved in my business ventures before then, either renting apartments or managing my properties, but nothing seemed to fit. He had the personality and the people skills for it, there was no question about that, but it turned out that all these young people moving to Brooklyn—many of them getting out from under their parents' roofs for the first time—didn't want some old guy barging in on them and telling them their bedroom looked like a pigsty. But put him in front of a classroom, and he was unstoppable.

The demand for Brooklyn rentals was still growing by the day, and Rapid Realty was growing along with it. Over 2004 and 2005, I poured hundreds of thousands of dollars into billboards, radio and TV spots, ads in newspapers, magazines and online, on buses and subway trains, basically getting the Rapid Realty name anywhere I thought someone in Brooklyn—or someone thinking about moving to Brooklyn—might see it.

The billboards alone became a side business for me. At first I rented existing billboard spaces, but that quickly became prohibitively expensive if I wanted to have enough money to advertise in other ways. The traditional billboard market wasn't working for me, so I created a new one. I approached landlords who had buildings in highly visible locations and offered to pay them a fee equivalent to their full real estate taxes for the year in one fell swoop if they would let me put a billboard on the side of their building. For the most part, these landlords had never been approached with any offer to put something on the side of their buildings, and they wouldn't have gone for it if they had. But the prospect of wiping out their real estate tax burden with a single stroke of a pen— that got their attention. Soon I had fifty of these billboards up on buildings all over New York, many of them right by highways or

major intersections. Before long, other advertisers were contacting me daily to ask if they could sublet the spaces, sometimes offering me in a single month what I'd paid the landlords for a full year.

All of these ads were aimed at finding new clients, of course, but they were also intended to bring in students for the real estate school, who would hopefully become new agents for Rapid Realty. The other real estate schools in town had relationships with older, bigger brokerage firms. I needed to draw business to my parents' school and create a source of potential agents for Rapid. The ads weren't anything fancy, just a simple, straightforward message: "Real estate classes, $200, get your license in one week," plus a phone number and website. It was everything you needed to know, and nothing else. And it worked.

The company was steadily growing. The days when we could all huddle around one computer seemed like a different lifetime, a different company. In fact, it wasn't long before I had to move my parents' real estate school into a larger location, in another building I bought around the corner, so I could turn that floor into more office space for Rapid Realty agents.

Soon, I renovated the third floor of the building, as well, changing it from apartments into even more office space. But I used this third floor space to do an experiment. At that point, I was already starting to think about expansion. I wondered: could someone else take the training techniques and infrastructure I'd developed and replicate it, turning a crop of brand new agents into a successful rental team that could compete with Rapid's veterans, all without me there to watch over everything?

To build and run this new team on the upper floor, I tapped a young, hotshot agent named Carlos Angelucci.

My Woz—Carlos Angelucci

How one good hire changed the course of Rapid Realty and set the stage for expansion

The first time I met the guy who would eventually become my closest friend and most trusted business partner, he was the mercilessly teased kid brother of two stellar employees. Little did I know, he would go on to become Rapid Realty's version of Steve Wozniak. Steve Jobs had Woz, and I had Carlos Angelucci.

I had hired one of his sisters to teach at my parents' real estate school. She was fantastic—fun, tough, smart, and best of all, she was the kind of teacher who would kick your ass if that's what it took to get you to study and pass the test so you could get your license. In other words, she got results. She was so great I ended up hiring her older sister to work as the school's receptionist. It didn't take long, though, before I realized that answering phones at the school all day was tragically underutilizing her talents, so I brought her on to work for me at Rapid Realty.

Although I initially brought her in to be the office's administrative assistant, she was almost immediately taking on duties far above and beyond that role, and knocking them out of the park. She became the office's go-to person for handling closing paper-

work, at one point closing 250 deals in a single month, while also managing the company payroll.

The Angelucci sisters had proven to be capable of handling anything I threw at them, and doing it with humor, intelligence, and a great attitude. So, naturally, I wanted to pull their baby brother, Carlos, into the company, as well.

I'd gotten to know Carlos a little just from hanging out with the Angelucci family. He already had a very solid job in retail management, making good money with a national brand that recognized they had a rising star on their hands (in fact, he was the youngest person in the whole company to hold his position). So, every time I tried to convince him to come join Rapid and become a real estate agent, he always politely told me no. And let me tell you, I used all my best recruiting tricks, like showing up in a Mercedes SL500 one day and a fully tricked-out Hummer the next, telling him about all my various businesses, my properties, everything I had going on, you name it. But Carlos liked the job he had, and he could see a future in it. He wasn't ready to throw all of that away to take a gamble on real estate, a field he knew virtually nothing about.

Gradually, though, I started to wear him down. It also helped that while I was trying to convince him from my side of things, his older sister, who was running payroll for Rapid Realty at the time, was telling him about how much money the top agents were making. Like me, she knew he could be great at real estate if he gave it a chance. Between the two of us, we got Carlos to come by the office a few times, and he was impressed by what he saw, particularly by the kind of work ethic he observed among the agents, no matter what time of day he came by. In the end, Carlos could tell this was a company that was primed to take off, and he knew he couldn't let an opportunity to get in on the ground floor just pass him by.

Carlos did what I consider the smartest possible move for anyone who's getting into real estate: he made it the center of his life. He quit his job (assuming he could probably get it back if this real estate thing didn't pan out) and he jumped into real estate with both feet, blowing through his classes and getting his license in a matter of weeks.

He came into Rapid Realty as a rental agent, ready to work day and night to master the business. But as much as I had wanted to get him into the company, and as glad as I was that he finally said yes, once he was there, I honestly cooled on him. His sisters were constantly cooing over him, pinching his cheeks and basically treating him like he was still a little kid they couldn't wait to show off. I was worried that I'd gone too far by bringing him in, that I'd reached the point of Angelucci Oversaturation, and now their sibling dynamic was going to take over the whole office. All their fussing over him and talking about how great he was wasn't making me think any more highly of him. I reserve my respect for people who earn it on their own merits.

In actuality, though, from the moment Carlos set foot into the Rapid Realty office as a licensed salesperson, he started producing deals, and soon he was performing as well as any of the top agents in the company.

Then came Rapid Realty's first real media appearance. A camera crew was coming to the office, and I had to personally select

the most articulate, intelligent, camera-ready agents to speak about the company. Again, the sisters pushed me to pick their amazing little brother, and again, all that did was make me want to keep him as far off camera as possible. But at the last minute, one of the agents I'd chosen got cold feet, and I needed someone to step up with practically no time to prepare. I was backed into a corner. No one else was willing to do it. What could I do? I gave Carlos a shot.

He absolutely blew me away. He talked about the company like he'd been working there since the day it opened. He spoke about the real estate market like he'd been working in the industry for a decade. He lived up to everything his sisters had been saying about him, and more.

After that rock star performance, I realized I needed to be paying close attention to this guy. I put Carlos on my team and gave him a daunting task: Rapid had the rights to a significant number of commercial listings, but no one was coming to us to lease them because we were only known as a residential rental brokerage. I wanted him to put together a catalogue of all our commercial listings, with a page of information on each one, and I gave him four hundred COMMERCIAL SPACE AVAILABLE signs to

hang on these properties. We would start getting the word out there that Rapid Realty handled commercial leasing, too.

Within thirty days, not only had Carlos created that catalogue and hung all four hundred signs, he had also built a whole team of agents under him just working on commercial deals, which were suddenly flying in around the clock. Clearly, even this was not enough of a challenge for Carlos.

That's when I decided to turn the third floor of the building into more office space. I wanted to see what Carlos was really capable of, and I wanted to begin testing the waters for a possible expansion of Rapid Realty at the same time.

I told Carlos that I would give him the run of the third floor. He could hire as many as fifty agents, and I'd give him a profit-sharing arrangement for any deals they generated. But he'd have to find them himself, hire them himself, and train them himself. I wanted him to compete against the company's existing trainer, who had already been doing this for years—in fact, he was the one who trained Carlos—to see whose agents could produce the most deals. The seasoned trainer would have all his current, fully trained agents, while Carlos would be starting completely from scratch.

The competition was ferocious. The company trainer didn't like being pitted against this upstart, and he pushed his team to the breaking point. Meanwhile Carlos, who started with nothing, began recruiting agents and designing his own training materials to help them go from beginners to experts as quickly as possible.

At the end of the competition, when the dust finally settled, the score was exactly tied. But the fact that Carlos had started at such a disadvantage—that he had built a team, trained them, and got them to produce as many deals as a team that was already fully formed and experienced before the competition even began—made him the clear winner in my eyes. I took a look at the job he'd done recruiting agents and the training materials he'd created for them, and I immediately appointed him Rapid Realty's new HR director.

One of his primary tasks in this new role was recruitment. We needed him to bring in as many quality applicants as possible and get them signed up for real estate classes. Once again, Carlos excelled. He had a novel approach to recruiting that got phenomenal results. Instead of just posting ads for real estate jobs, or just targeting salespeople, he went after people in other fields who had skills that could easily translate into sales—actors, bartenders, waiters—anyone who needed people skills to be successful. Soon he was bringing in so many recruits that instead of interviewing them one at a time, he'd hold open houses where he could walk a group of potential recruits through the office at once, teaching them about the company and about real estate, all while simultaneously evaluating them all as they went along.

He was bringing in so many recruits that we soon had to start chartering buses to drive them six-plus hours upstate to testing facilities so they could take their licensing exams. There were only a couple of testing sites in the city, and they booked up so early that it could take weeks for someone who had completed their real estate classes to actually be able to take their mandatory state exam. But Carlos's recruits were so excited to begin their real estate careers that they were willing to line up outside the Rapid Realty office at two in the morning on a Tuesday and drive up to Rochester or Albany, where it was easier to get a seat for an exam, just so they could get their licenses that much faster.

Soon Carlos became one of my chief strategists. That rise was in part due to a few other senior people leaving the company, but it was also largely because he and I were on the same wavelength when it came to business. Like me, he had an unshakable work ethic, a powerful inner drive, and the belief that sleep could wait until we were either very rich or extremely dead.

Things Fall Apart

How I achieved a dream, but lost a hero—
and almost lost my company

In the midst all of this growth and excitement and hustling, I never lost sight of the promise I'd made my mother when I was six: to buy her a big, white mansion where our whole family could live. In 2005, I finally purchased a property in Bay Ridge, Brooklyn. It cost well over a million dollars, and it would cost millions more to turn it into the custom-designed mansion I'd been envisioning and gradually refining in my head all this time. The construction would take years, but it was finally underway.

Unfortunately, my father never got to see the finished product. He was a smoker for much of his adult life, and although he quit when I was in elementary school, the years of damage finally caught up with him. In November 2006, at the age of seventy-eight, his lung collapsed. The doctors did everything they could, but ultimately his body couldn't get enough oxygen and his organs started to fail. He died a few days later.

I think it's natural, when you lose someone close to you like that, to ask yourself if you should have spent more time with them. Between my rental properties and Rapid Realty, I had been working so hard, seven days a week, often going months at a time without taking a day off. Yes, it was all working toward the ultimate goal of providing a better life for my parents, but now my father wasn't even going to get to enjoy the benefits. Was it all a waste?

The more I thought about it, though, the more I realized that no, it hadn't been a waste at all. I'd given him the ability to spend the last few years of his life doing what he wanted to do. He had spent his whole career in the classroom to make ends meet, and when he retired from that, he had to go right back out and spend his nights walking the city with a bird on his shoulder. In his last few years he returned to the classroom, but not because he had to. He did it because he loved it, and he did it at a school that he owned, that his son built for him. And even as hard as I'd been working, I'd spent a huge amount of quality time with him over those years since his retirement from his Bird Man act. And while my father might never have had the chance to live in the house I was building, he got to see it under construction. He passed away

knowing that I was going to take care of my mother, that we were both going to be okay.

My father taught me a lot of lessons that I'll carry with me for the rest of my life, but the biggest one by far was the importance of hard work. There was no better way to honor him than to pick myself up and get back on that horse.

But almost as soon as I went back to work, disaster struck. Rapid Realty's computer systems suffered a massive failure. We lost years of data, including information about hundreds, if not thousands, of apartments and commercial spaces, as well as the contact information for our clientele of landlords and management companies. It was just about the most catastrophic sort of loss a real estate company can suffer. Not only had we lost our inventory, we'd lost a lot of our capacity to quickly replenish that inventory. It would be embarrassing enough to have to call up all of our landlords and say, "Sorry, I lost the information about every apartment you trusted us to list for you. Can you resend me all that info?" But how are you even supposed to do that when you don't have the landlord's phone number anymore?

Thankfully, between me and my agents, we had enough information written down to begin piecing back together some of our listings and a portion of our landlord client list, but I resolved never to let a data loss like that happen again. I brought on a technology officer and began designing a proprietary database for Rapid Realty that would be vastly more secure while also offering a wide array of cutting-edge technology solutions to make our agents' lives easier and boost productivity.

I also wanted this new database to be something that would link any future Rapid Realty offices. I didn't just want Rapid Realty to bounce back from our data loss, I wanted it to rise up better than ever. It was time to expand. I spent much of 2007 hand-selecting and personally training some of the company's top brokers to step into the crucial role as managers of the first wave of new Rapid Realty branches. They were excited. I was excited. I had

no idea that I was setting the stage for the darkest period in the company's history.

When the housing bubble burst toward the end of 2007, demand for rentals skyrocketed. That's one of the things that make rentals such a stable investment—when the economy plummets, the rental industry actually gets stronger. It was a difficult time for the country, but for Rapid Realty, the timing couldn't have been any better to expand. Our services had never been more necessary. But then, just before we were supposed to sign leases for the first branch office, the broker I had trained to manage it told me that he was leaving the company to start his own competing firm. And then another one of the managers told me the same thing. And then another. And another.

All told, seven of my most highly trained brokers left Rapid Realty to start their own companies, using the knowledge and techniques that I taught them, including the specialized training I'd been giving them to prepare them to run an office. I had trained my own competition.

That would have been bad enough, but when these brokers left, they didn't go quietly. They took dozens of other agents with them, poaching them away from Rapid Realty with promises of sky-high commission splits and unrealistic benefits. Even after they left, they would bombard our remaining agents with phone calls, texts, and emails, trying to lure them away with promises they could never keep. We had to start training our agents how to respond to these attempts.

And then came the smear campaigns.

It wasn't enough to leave Rapid Realty in the lurch or drain our workforce. These agents-turned-competitors wanted to make sure they didn't have to fight Rapid for listings. They went online and posted hundreds of fraudulent reviews posing as customers and claiming all sorts of horrible things about Rapid on all the major review sites. They were doing everything in their power to destroy our reputation. They would even contact landlords and lie about Rapid Realty to try to deter them from wanting to list

their properties with us. It was relentless. And, as anyone who has ever had anything negative posted about them online knows all too well, it doesn't matter if it's true or not—once something's out there, it's incredibly difficult to get rid of it.

In some cases we could prove that these online reviews were false and get them taken down. We even had to take some of these former agents to court when we were able to prove that we were being targeted for slander, or that our clients or agents were being harassed. But it's never possible to get rid of everything. And even if you could, the problem with a negative review is, once someone sees it, the damage is already done. If you look up a restaurant online and see a reviewer claiming they got food poisoning, are you really going to check back in a week to see if that review got removed for making a false claim? Of course not—you're just going to find somewhere else to eat.

The temptation when something like this happens is to give into the negativity and strike back, to attack these people just like they're attacking you. But I made a conscious choice to stay out of the mud. I wanted Rapid Realty to be better than that. We weren't going to spread lies about our competitors or poach their agents. We were just going to focus on doing our job to the best of our ability. So, we defended ourselves when we could prove we had the legal high ground, and the rest of the time we focused on rebuilding our brand.

Bigger and Better

How Rapid Realty rose from the ashes,
and the birth of the Lolli Mansion

In 2008, in the midst of all my would-be managers leaving the company to start their own competing firms, I took the opportunity to reorganize. The first thing I did was promote Carlos Angelucci to chief operating officer. He had already become my right-hand man by that point, and an invaluable leader to the company, so this was just a way to make it official. We put our heads together to rework Rapid Realty's commission structure. This, plus our newly implemented database, breathed new life into the company. Despite the losses to our staff, we soon grew to over a hundred agents. We had to turn the top floor of the building into more office space, and agents still had to fight one another for workstations.

Although we'd lost our first crop of managers and their nasty exit stung me to the core, I was still determined to expand as soon as possible to capitalize on the booming demand for rentals. All over the city, real estate companies much larger and older than Rapid Realty were closing down offices or cutting their staff because they were exclusively focused on sales, and no one was buying. No other company could match Rapid Realty in terms of rental expertise and experience, but we had to make our move soon. There was already word of some of these bigger firms gearing up to launch rental divisions, and our advantage wouldn't last forever.

We took a long, hard look at our remaining veteran agents and found several we felt were ready to step up to the challenge of managing a branch. These were maybe agents who I had passed over the first time around because I thought they weren't quite ready at the time, maybe they'd make good candidates for the second wave of expansion. But they were all stepping up to the plate in terms of taking on responsibilities and closing deals now that so many of Rapid's former top agents had left, and it had me seeing them in a new light.

That's when I happened to run into an old friend who owned a rubbish removal company. We got to talking and he started going on and on about the merits of franchising.

Any business owner who wants to open multiple locations has to make the big decision: do I open corporate-owned branches and retain more control, or do I give up some control and franchise? Franchising can mean quicker growth, but it also takes a lot of complex planning and organization, and more than that, it means giving up ownership of your new offices and entrusting more of your brand's reputation to other people. Remember, I'm the guy

who had a hard time hiring a secretary. Letting other people own branches of my brand outright? Not a chance.

Still, I couldn't stop thinking about it. And the more I thought about it, the more it made sense. My managers had left to open their own firms. And it's not like that was the first time in real estate history that something like that happened. In fact, it's so common that some real estate industry magazines run recurring columns just listing all the recent notable departures as high-ranking agents jump ship from one company to start their own or take a higher position somewhere else.

It should come as no surprise that people who excel as real estate agents also tend to be ambitious. You must have that fire if you're going to get out there and chase those commissions every day. So maybe it's not shocking that a lot of top agents would want to own their own firms. After all, that's exactly what I did, wasn't it? So why should I expect any different from the people who worked for me?

Franchising would mean giving up control, and it would mean giving up a bigger slice of the company's commissions. But it could also mean keeping my best people under the Rapid Realty umbrella and offering them a much quicker and easier path to business ownership than they'd have if they struck out on their own. It would be win-win, at least in theory.

Carlos and I started discussing franchising as a serious option. It seemed to have potential, but I still wasn't entirely sold on the idea. But while I was mulling over my options, the dream that I had been pursuing since I was six years old finally came true.

At long last, the construction was finally complete on the big, white mansion I'd promised my mother twenty-four years earlier, and we were able to move in. True to my vision, it was large enough for the whole family. My mother had an entire self-contained apartment on the first floor, while the second floor was my living space and the third held my home office. I put love and care into every detail of the house, from the rich color of the hardwood floors to the wrought-iron banister along the grand staircase, which ascended alongside a three-story wall of glass. But it wasn't enough for the house to be beautiful; I wanted it to be fun and functional, too. I made sure there were big spaces for entertaining, including a billiards lounge, a private movie theater, and, of course, the pool with hot tub, fountains, and built-in flat-screen TV (and let me tell you, once you've watched the game while floating in your own pool, nothing else will do).

The house soon became known as the Lolli Mansion. People sometimes give me a hard time about it. "Oh sure, Anthony, go ahead and name it after yourself." But I never saw it that way. To me, calling it the Lolli Mansion is just honoring what it was always meant to be: my gift to my family. It was always for them. It still is.

Moving into the mansion was bittersweet. On the one hand, I felt my father's absence in every corner of the house. Not having him there was hard, although I like to think he was there in spirit. On the other hand, it was the realization of my entire life's work up to that point, the completion of the goal that had motivated me since I was a kid. And seeing the look on my mother's face as she explored the beautiful home her son had built for her, just like he swore he would, well...if I had to sacrifice, if I had to overcome obstacles, if I had to push myself to the brink, that look made it all worth it.

The Lolli Mansion would go on to become a part of the Rapid Realty brand. Many Rapid Realty franchisees would take their first steps on the path to business ownership by reading manuals underneath the customized, starlike lights of the movie theater. Company meetings and parties at the house became a regular occurrence. But the Lolli Mansion would also become a brand unto itself, and actually enable me to branch out into the entertainment industry. Shows on FOX, NBC, and CBS have all toured the property. It's been the backdrop for music videos, films, and photo shoots. On my birthday one year, Spike Lee even came over and screened a movie with me and the group of friends I'd invited over to celebrate.

Energized by the achievement of one major life goal, I was

ready to tackle another. It was time to take Rapid Realty to the big leagues. Carlos and I got on a plane and flew to Chicago to learn everything we could about the world of franchising.

They say we're living in the Information Age, and it's easy to see why. We have so much information available to us at our fingertips. But a consequence of that bombardment of information is that it's far too easy to just skim, and not really think critically about what you're seeing. If you take only one thing away from me, let it be this: when it comes to major moments, whether in life or in business, always put in the time to learn before you leap. I've said it before and I'll say it again—if you're not setting yourself up to succeed, you're setting yourself up to fail. And success means learning.

We spent months learning the ins and outs of turning a business into a franchise from some of the world's leading experts on the subject. We studied hundreds of other franchise companies to learn from their models and mistakes. We employed one of the nation's premiere franchising teams to help us generate our agreements and structure. After a year of painstaking preparation, then, and only then, we felt we were ready to test the waters.

In early 2009, we set up a test franchise in Crown Heights, an up-and-coming neighborhood that didn't have the cachet and built-in rental interest of an area like Park Slope or Williamsburg, and we chose an office space around the corner from a homeless shelter, in an out-of-the-way spot that wouldn't benefit from a lot of foot traffic. With the demand for rentals being what it was, I had no doubt that a rental-based real estate office would do well if we stuck it in the middle of a hot neighborhood. I wanted to see how a Rapid Realty franchise would do if I didn't give it any advantages at all. I set up one of the brokers I'd been grooming to be a manager as the test franchisee and I sat back to watch what happened.

Within a few months, the pilot franchise had blown past all the benchmarks I'd set for it. There was no doubt left in my mind. Franchising was the future of Rapid Realty. In August 2009, the agent I'd put in charge of the test franchise became Rapid Realty's

first official franchisee, opening an office in Bay Ridge, just blocks from the Lolli Mansion.

With Great Growth Comes Great Possibility

How Rapid Realty's meteoric growth raised money for cancer research and led to people getting tattoos

Even as the economy started to show signs of stabilizing, the strength and size of the rental market only increased. Lenders were still wary about giving out loans, even to well-qualified candidates, and people were understandably mistrustful of the mortgage industry. Studies showed a quickly growing number of people said they would prefer to rent for their entire lives, even if they could afford to buy a home.

All this demand for rentals directly fueled a demand for Rapid Realty franchises. Within eighteen months, we had opened over forty new franchises all over Brooklyn and beyond, spreading out into the other boroughs. At a time when jobs were scarce, we started providing our aspiring agents with discounted and even free tuition to real estate school to help them get their salesperson's licenses. I hated the idea that anyone out there might be prevented from starting a new career path because they couldn't afford the classes. And unlike most other real estate companies, we didn't turn away prospective agents because they were too young, or because they didn't look or sound the way people supposedly expected agents to look or sound. That was actually a core premise of Rapid Realty right from the start. I wanted it to be a company that gave people a chance.

With all those new offices recruiting agents, and our welcoming, inclusive hiring policies, Rapid Realty soon grew to a staff of nearly a thousand, making it one of the largest real estate companies in New York City.

I was no stranger to hard work at this point, but this was operating on a whole new level. Working with new and aspiring franchisees soon took over my day-to-day responsibilities. It wasn't uncommon for me to put in a twenty-hour day and spend all of it training new franchisees, scouting for locations for new offices, meeting with landlords and negotiating leases on franchisees' behalf, helping them draw up designs for layouts or signage, picking out furniture and fixtures, helping a franchisee finish the final coat of paint on their office to get ready in time for their grand opening, and then going back home to answer questions from the group of agents who had just spent the day reading in my in-home movie theater to decide if opening a Rapid Realty franchise was right for them. And then I'd do it all again the next day.

I was running around so much, I didn't have time to devote to overseeing Rapid Realty's flagship office, let alone actually doing any apartment renting myself. Ultimately, I converted the top two floors of the original office back into apartments and turned the ground-floor storefront into a franchise as well. I won't lie, that one was tough. Even though that office has been out of my hands for a few years now, anytime I drop by, it still feels like my baby.

All that growth brought new attention and new accolades. New York media outlets started following Rapid Realty, and not just the ones that focus on real estate. Anytime a real estate-related story broke in the news, someone wanted me to comment. In 2012, Rapid Realty NYC debuted on the Inc. 5000, marking it as one of the fastest-growing companies in America. Franchisee Satisfaction awards from the Franchise Business Review soon followed. In 2013, the Golden Bridge Awards named me Entrepreneur of the Year, which felt pretty good considering that award typically went to the heads of tech companies, and had previously been given to Mark Zuckerberg for a little startup called Facebook. But none of the attention could prepare me for the bizarre turn of events that was about to unfold.

It all started back in 2011, when an agent named Adam from Rapid's Bushwick franchise helped a tattoo artist find a new space for his shop. The artist was so impressed by Adam that he offered to give him a tattoo of the Rapid Realty logo. Adam was heavily tattooed already and didn't mind the idea of one more, so he agreed. Just before the artist got to work, Adam gave me a call to let me know what he was about to do.

I rushed down there to see it with my own eyes. I ended up getting a video of the whole thing. On it, Adam explained that he was about to face his first winter as an agent. Winter is typically the slower season for real estate, and it's when a lot of new agents give up on the business. He said he thought this tattoo would keep him motivated.

I was blown away by this incredible display of loyalty to the company and to the profession. I asked Adam what I could give him in return, but he laughed it off. I was serious, though, and in the end, since he had made such a permanent commitment to the brand I'd started, I offered to permanently boost him to the company's highest commission split. It wasn't anything he couldn't have achieved on his own—agents could reach that split by bringing in deals, promoting the company on social media, or even by volunteering for charity—but it was the best I could think of.

I shared the video with the whole company, but other than making for a fun subject of conversation around the office for a little while, I thought that was that. But the following summer, two more agents from a different office, inspired by the video, decided to get their own tattoos of the Rapid logo. Again, I was blown away, and again, I offered to permanently boost their commission splits to the company's highest level.

It was one of those agents who suggested that I extend the

same offer to the entire company. So I did, thinking maybe there might be one or two more agents out there who would take me up on it. It turned out there were a lot more than that. On one day in August 2012, eleven agents from different offices all met up and got Rapid Realty tattoos together. By the following spring the number of tattooed agents had reached forty. (Today the number is over a hundred.)

That spring was when the real estate news site Inman ran a contest on their Twitter feed asking companies to submit their most unusual marketing ideas. I had never thought about the tattoos as a marketing tool, but there was no denying they had that effect. When you see someone walking around with their company's logo etched into their arm, you're going to want to know more.

One well-crafted tweet from Rapid Realty's communications director later, we won the contest. Inman published a short article about our tattooed agents. Then that article got picked up by the Drudge Report. Then our local CBS affiliate. And then, well, pretty much everybody.

I later spoke with an outside media consultant who estimated that the story received roughly twenty million dollars' worth of media coverage in the first two weeks alone. It was in newspapers, it was on TV, on the radio, online. It was everywhere. I was doing interviews by phone with radio stations in France and interviews via satellite for an Australian morning show. One day I was on *The Today Show* with one of our tattooed agents, and that night, in one of his final opening monologues before stepping down as host of *The Tonight Show*, Jay Leno joked about the story, cutting away to a bald cameraman who had a fake tattoo of the show's logo on the front of his head, and then turned around to show a tattoo reading "With Jimmy Fallon" on the back.

All the press was so fast and furious that it felt totally surreal. Half the stories reported that the company was giving out 15 percent raises for the tattoos, which wasn't exactly true, but it had taken on a life of its own at that point. In the end, Rapid Realty ended up winning a PR World award for Viral Marketing Campaign of the Year, which was a nice bonus for something that didn't start as marketing, and that we didn't actually try to make viral.

All that recognition opened doors for the company, enabling us to spread beyond New York. By the end of 2013 we had opened offices in Boston and San Diego. One of the San Diego franchisees even got a Rapid Realty tattoo on the floor of the West Coast Franchising Expo. (At one point I got a letter from a guy in Brazil who wanted to open a Rapid Realty franchise down there, and who offered to get a tattoo of our logo to show how serious he was. I declined.)

I even found that the publicity from the tattoo story had an impact on my property investment. Suddenly, when I'd approach a seller or sit down with a bank, they would light up with recognition. They knew who I was, they knew what I did, and they knew the kind of excitement I could generate. It made them that much more eager to work with me. It was like when I was first starting out in the real estate business, only now instead of being the Bird Man's Kid, I was the Tattoo CEO.

• • •

One of the things that makes me the proudest of Rapid Realty's growth is that the bigger the company has become, the more we've been able to give back. I'd always tried to make giving back to the community a vital part of the company. In the early days, I'd gather up the entire staff and we'd pile into a van and go spend an afternoon volunteering at a coat drive, or delivering baskets full of food to needy families on the night before Thanksgiving. Now the days of fitting the whole company into a van were long gone, but that opened up other possibilities.

Since the company became a franchise, we've taken on bigger projects like organizing comedy shows to raise money for the American Cancer Society or participating in Habitat for Humanity builds or fielding teams in the NYC AIDS Walk, but it's also been wonderful to see the individual offices rallying together to support

charities of their own choosing. The breadth and diversity of the people who work at Rapid Realty has introduced me to a wide array of terrific causes that I never would have known about otherwise.

The diversity of Rapid Realty is actually one of my favorite things about the company. Because each new franchise recruits agents from its surrounding neighborhood, our company is every bit as diverse as the cities we serve. And when people from so many different backgrounds and experiences feel they can come to me and share the causes that make them passionate, that's a wonderful thing.

All told, we've been able to support over seventy different charitable organizations, and that number is only growing. I love having a beautiful house, I love driving a fancy car, I love wearing a nice watch. But for a poor kid from Brooklyn, being able to help so many people is the part of being successful that I love the most.

Between growing Rapid Realty and seeking out new investment properties and opportunities, I've gotten to travel all across the country and around the world. One thing that always amazes me is that, wherever I go, I constantly bump into former Rapid Realty agents. They recognize me or Carlos on the street, and they come running up to shake our hands and thank us for giving them a chance. Many of them are still working in real estate; they just moved somewhere Rapid Realty doesn't have an office (yet). Others have left real estate entirely for careers as varied as law enforcement, firefighting, performing, teaching, even scientific research.

The one thing they all have in common is this: Rapid Realty gave them their first big chance. That's what they always want to tell me: Rapid Realty gave them an opportunity when they were eighteen, nineteen, twenty years old and nobody else would give them the time of day. And even if they didn't stick with real estate—even if real estate was just something they did to put themselves through school, and they never had any plans to make it their lifelong career—working at Rapid gave them confidence, the training, and the skills to go on and do something great with their lives.

When I look at Rapid Realty, at all the agents who were able to embark on new careers, all the people who were able to become business owners, all the amazing things that we've been able to accomplish, I can't help thinking the same thing I think when I look at the Lolli Mansion: this is the house that real estate built.

That's the power of this business. It's the power to change not only your life, but your family's life, and the lives of those around you.

Everyone has their own personal definition of success. Me, I'm the sort of person where I don't know if I'll ever be able to stop moving. I used to be moving toward building a home for my family. Then it was expanding my company. As I write this, I'm working toward building Rapid Realty to a hundred offices. But I know it can go so much further than that. I want Rapid Realty to be a household name across America.

If all of this was possible for me, then it's possible for you, too. But make no mistake, it doesn't come easy.

I've lived my life by this ethos: Work like others won't so you can live like others can't. Most people will read that and just nod or laugh it off. But if you're truly willing to put in the work, if you truly have the dedication and the drive to give this business everything you've got, then there's no limit to how far you can go.

PART 2

The Path to Success

Before you embark on any new venture—I don't care if it's real estate or making hats—you need to prepare yourself for success. That means creating good habits right out of the gate. There's no sense in saying, "I'll just jump in and see how it goes first, and then if I like it, I'll get serious about it." If you're not serious about it from the start, you won't produce results. And if you're not producing results, you won't like it. And even if you manage to keep going, you'll be developing bad habits, so by the time you do decide to get serious, you'll have to retrain yourself how to do the job right.

That sort of mentality is bad news in any business, but in a commission-based business it's absolute poison. Do yourself—and more importantly, your future self—a favor and start out right.

Get Yourself Motivated

Unlocking your own productivity through the power of goals and visualization

Let's take a minute to talk about goals.

I've said before how promising my mother when I was six years old that I'd buy her a big, white mansion one day gave me something to work toward, and how having that goal motivated me throughout the early days of my career. But just as importantly—maybe even more importantly—it helped me develop the

habit of visualizing and setting goals early on in life, so I didn't have to force myself to create that habit later.

The things we learn as kids get ingrained in us and are always easier to stick to than the things we learn as adults. But that doesn't mean that if you're not already in the habit of setting clear goals for yourself, it's too late to start. Actually, today's the perfect time. You know why? Because today might not be as good as having already developed a good habit yesterday, but it's twenty-four entire hours better than doing it tomorrow.

At any given moment, you should have three goals in mind: one **short-term**, one **medium-term**, and one **long-term**. Having more than one in any particular category is fine, but you should have at least one of each, and you should always be aware of what they are. That way, whenever you come to a professional crossroads, you can always ask yourself, "Would this get me closer to one of my goals?" If the answer is yes, go for it. If the answer is no, it's probably not the path for you. Having that simple mental checkbox to use can help you breeze through some of the toughest career decisions you'll ever have to face.

Your goals will change and evolve over time. Your long-term goals will eventually become medium-term goals as the pieces you need to accomplish them begin to click into place, and then they become short-term goals as you put them into motion, until finally you achieve them. For instance, my first long-term goal was to buy a mansion for my family. Although I set that goal when I was six, I wasn't able to really start working toward it until I was old enough to get a job. But then, every job I tried, I always asked myself, "Is this going to help me buy that mansion?" As long as the answer was no, my heart wasn't really in it, which is why I didn't really connect with a career path until I tried real estate.

As I started to do well, and particularly after I started my own company and that began to take off, that goal went from long- to medium-term as it started to become a financial possibility. Then, once I had the money and all that stood between me and my dream was the construction, it became a short-term goal.

Note that, in this case, my short-term goal—the actual build-ing of the mansion—still took another three years to complete. That's an important point. Your short-term goal isn't something that you can wake up and scratch off your list in a single day. It's something that you can get up and directly work toward on a given day.

It's also important to note that, as my long-term goal moved closer and closer, I was replacing it with new goals at each step. Expanding Rapid Realty, growing to a certain number of offices, acquiring new properties to generate a target amount in passive income each month—all of these have been my long-term goal at one time or another. Since starting my company and buying my first investment property, I've always had goals for each side of my professional life.

For instance, if you were to ask me, right now as I'm writing this, what my goals are for Rapid Realty, I'd tell you:

- My **short-term goal** is to open five more franchises, which are all under development right now in three different states. That's what I worked on today.
- My **medium-term goal** is to open one hundred Rapid Realty offices.
- My **long-term goal** is to make Rapid Realty a house-hold name all across America. Whenever someone moves to a new city and needs an apartment, I want them to say, "I should go find a Rapid Realty office."

So you can see how working on my short-term goal benefits my medium-term goal, which benefits my long-term goal.

Of course, at this point in my career, my professional goals are not solely tied to Rapid Realty. I have a separate company for managing my portfolio of properties, which I am constantly work-ing on expanding and improving, and that comes with its own set of ever-evolving goals.

On top of that, my success as a broker, CEO, and investor has become a brand, and that brand has opened up paths to me

that would have been closed off earlier in my career: My property investment has led to property development. My success with Rapid Realty's database and winning the Golden Bridge Award has led to opportunities developing real estate software and apps. My media exposure has led to public speaking opportunities and allowed me to branch out into the entertainment industry. Even the simple fact that I grew my company through franchising has opened doors for me. Franchising is an industry unto itself, and because of all that I've accomplished in that arena, franchisors and aspiring franchisors seek me out to consult on their growing brands, even ones that have nothing to do with real estate at all. Each of these paths is a venture that I'm currently exploring, and each one comes with its own set of goals. (And, as I write this, I'm a new dad, which is sure to come with its own set of lifelong goals, but that's a whole other book.)

So, let's say you want to follow my lead—you want to get a real estate license, become a broker, and use the money you earn from renting and selling properties to finance the purchase of investment properties—and your big dream is to become a millionaire. In that case, a good initial set of goals might look like this:

- **Short-term:** Get your real estate salesperson's license.
- **Medium-term:** Buy your first investment property.
- **Long-term:** Make your first million.

Along the way, you'd have a lot of smaller, short-term goals. Getting your real estate license might take you a week to a month or more. Once you get it, you might want to focus on landing your first deal, then landing a certain number of deals each month, or making a certain amount in commissions each month, until you get to where you need to be to be able to buy that first building.

Now, making a million bucks might not be the big dream that motivates you. It wasn't for me, although I'd be lying if I said that making my first million wasn't a big moment in my career. I used making a million dollars as an example because a nice, round dollar amount is easy to get excited about. But I actually think that

the best long-term goals aren't about making a specific amount of money. If everything you do is just working toward a target figure, once you reach it, what do you have? Just a nice figure on a bank statement. There's nothing wrong with that, but I think it's far more motivational to work toward something more concrete. That's where visualization comes in.

What does success mean to you?

That's not a rhetorical question. I really mean it. What is your version of success? What does it look like? What does it feel like? Having a million bucks is great, but it doesn't mean anything if you don't spend it. What are you working toward?

For me, it was building a white mansion big enough for my whole family. I thought about it every day. What does your mansion look like? How many rooms does it have? Where would you relax? Where would you entertain? What sort of special touches would it have?

Or maybe your version of success is owning a Porsche. What would it feel like to sit behind the wheel? What would the engine sound like? How would the interior smell the first time you got inside?

Maybe it's being able to take a trip around the world with the person you love. Where would you go? How would you travel? What sorts of things would you do? What sorts of dishes would you eat? Where would you stay?

Take a minute to really visualize your own personal version of success. Don't worry about what anyone else thinks success is. I want you to define it for yourself. Really think about it. Use all five senses. Form a complete picture.

Seriously. Put the book down and do it. It's okay, I'll be here when you get back.

Got it? Do you have a picture in your head? Good. That's your long-term goal.

Hold on to that image. I want you to think about it daily. I want you to call that image to mind when you celebrate your successes, to remind you what the big picture is, and what you're really working toward. I want you to call that image to mind when things are at their hardest to give you that push you need on the days when you don't think you can even get out of bed.

That image may change somewhat over time, and that's okay. I started visualizing my mansion when I was six years old—how much do you think I really knew back then about designing a house? The fact that I had to take out the backyard petting zoo and the trampoline room doesn't make the vision a failure, because it still got me where I wanted to go.

It's not important that your vision remains exactly the same over time, just so long as it's changing because you want it to—because your concept of success is evolving—and not because you lost sight of the prize. Likewise, it's not important if the reality of what you achieve doesn't exactly match what you envisioned all along. If you get into that Porsche and the leather doesn't smell like you imagined it would, are you going to trade it in for a used Subaru and call the whole thing a wash? I don't think so.

All that's important is that it motivates you. Because staying motivated is so important in any business venture, but especially when it comes to real estate, which can often be feast or famine. There will be times when it seems like all you need to do is wake up in the morning to land a deal. But there may also be times when it feels like nothing is going your way, and in those moments, you need to find the motivation not just to keep going, but to go even harder. That's what your vision is for. Keep focused on your vision, and your vision will keep you focused.

Of course, if you're reading this, you're a human being, and human beings have limited memories, limited attention spans, and a far more limited ability to focus on multiple things at once than a lot of people would like to admit. You're not going to be able to keep your vision in mind at all times, and there will be days when it's hard to remember what you're working toward at all. That's why I strongly recommend giving yourself some help in the form of a visual aid. My suggestion is to make a **vision board**—a bulletin board, or even a piece of poster board, that you can cover with images that inspire you to pursue your long-term goal. It could be pictures of the car you want to drive, the places you want to go, the things you want to do, or pictures of houses, rooms, or even single pieces of furniture that you'd want for yourself. Whatever images remind you of why you're doing what you're doing, that's what goes on the board. Then you put it in your bedroom, or somewhere you'll see it every day as a constant source of inspiration and motivation.

These days, apps like Pinterest make it easy to create a virtual vision board that you can add to with the click of a button. That's great, but I still encourage you to make a physical one. Take it from someone who has both hired construction crews to renovate my buildings and renovated them with my own two hands—you have a much stronger connection to the things you build yourself.

I know some of you reading this will roll your eyes at the idea of a vision board. You might think it's a bunch of New Age bullshit, or that you're too old to be doing some arts and crafts project, or that you don't need physical reminders to keep your vision in mind. Let me tell you, if that's your attitude, it's time to get over yourself. I know a lot of successful people—men and women, from different backgrounds, including some ex-military—who would tell you that creating a vision board for themselves was the smartest move they ever made, and that they credit it for keeping them on the path that led to their success.

I'd also guess that the real reason you're hesitant about doing it is that you're embarrassed; you think someone will see it and make fun of you for it. Well, first of all, if the people in your life who might see it wouldn't be supportive of the fact that you're doing everything you can to keep yourself focused on achieving your financial dreams, you might need to reevaluate the people you're spending your time with. And second, if feeling a little self-conscious is going to stop you from going after what you want, you're never going to get it. Success comes to people who put themselves out there.

But if you really can't bring yourself to make a vision board, if you really don't have the private space or the supportive environment to make and display something like that, then at the bare minimum, when you choose your goals, be sure to write them down. Write them in clear, big letters and put the list somewhere you'll see it every single day: by your bathroom mirror, by your alarm clock, by your computer, wherever you know you'll have to look at it.

Study after study has shown that writing down your goals increases the likelihood that you'll achieve them. It's not magic—it's not like writing down *I want a Lamborghini* will make one suddenly appear in your driveway—it's simply that committing your goals to paper and giving yourself that simple visual reminder helps you stay focused on the steps you need to take to pursue them. It's the simplest thing in the world to do, and it has practically guaranteed results. If you can't do this one tiny but crucial thing to give yourself the boost you deserve, then maybe it's time to scale down your dreams. But I don't think you want to do that. And believe me, I don't want you to do it either.

Trust Your Heart, Trust Your Gut

When do you follow your heart, and when
do you follow your instincts?

"Follow your heart."

I'd be pretty surprised to find that I was the first person to give you that particular piece of advice. You've probably heard it all your life in regards to your career, education, love life, hobbies, you name it. In most cases, people probably used it to mean you should pursue your passion, do what really moves you. That's good advice, and you should absolutely stick to it. But I want you to think about that phrase in a different way.

When I tell you to follow your heart in business, I mean you should do what you're passionate about, sure, but I also mean you should do what makes you feel good—and just as importantly,

you should back away from decisions that make you feel like a crappy person.

Don't worry, this isn't the part where I try to push you into giving to charity, although you should—as soon as you can, as often as you can, in whatever way you can. This also isn't the part where I tell you that it's better to help people than to make money. It's okay, you can do both. In fact, you can do a lot of both.

What I mean is this: in any business—and especially in something as sensitive and important as real estate—you will inevitably find yourself in a situation where you could make more money by screwing someone over than you could by helping someone out. I'm not going to sit here and tell you that you should take a loss. If you provided a service, you deserve to be compensated. But I'm saying there's a difference between taking a loss and taking a smaller win in order to do right by someone.

Let me give you an example from my own life. I recently purchased a property from a woman who'd been having a tough go of it. I'm not going to walk you through every lousy hand life ever dealt her, but suffice it to say that by the time I met her, she had nothing to her name but this run-down building, which was falling apart around her ears. The building needed to be torn down and rebuilt from the ground up, but the property was in a hot location.

A number of parties were circling around her, trying to swindle her out of the building for far less than it was worth. I could have been one of them; I could have charmed her into selling it to me on the cheap and laughed all the way to the bank. It wouldn't have been hard to make her think she was getting a good deal and then forget about her. Once the deal's done and the deed is in my hands, who cares, right?

Except that if I had done that, I would have felt like a scumbag. That's the sort of thing that sticks with you and leaves its stink all over everything you touch. I might not sleep that much, but when I do, I like to enjoy it. So instead, I offered her a fair price for the building and made her a promise: once I renovated it, I'd hold one of the apartments for her at a rate she'd easily be able to handle, and she'd have a place to live for the rest of her life.

Now, even if the purchase price was the same, I would have stood to make more money over the lifetime of the investment if I pushed her out and rented the renovated apartment at the market rate, like every other unit in the building. Instead, it will take me a little longer to recoup my investment, and my ultimate profit from this building might be a little lower, but make no mistake: I will still recoup that investment and make a profit. And now I've also given a nice lady who's had a rough life some stability and security that will last her the rest of her days. And I sleep like a baby.

All I'm saying is, when you come to a crossroads where one option might make you more money, but makes you feel dirty, while the other option means making less but liking the face in the mirror a little more, I've always gone with the second option, and it's worked out pretty well for me so far.

Now, the second big piece of cliché advice, after "follow your heart," is "trust your gut." This, too, is a cliché because it's true. Your gut is the best friend you could have in business.

When you're facing a tough decision, and you get that feeling deep in your core that's pulling you one way or another, that way is always the right choice. That feeling is your body telling you to face up to a hard truth. If you think about a situation long enough, you can always rationalize your way out of any choice. But your gut always knows the right call, and most of the time it knows right from the start.

Many a sleepless night can be avoided if you just take the time to listen to what your gut is telling you. That's your instincts talking. We are taught from the time we're kids to think about things logically, and that's usually the way to go. But when you spend night after sleepless night staring at the ceiling, trying to convince yourself that your logic is correct, even though it just feels wrong—that's a sign that you could have saved yourself a lot of trouble by just trusting your gut.

So, what do you do when your heart says one thing and

your gut says another? Situations like that are, sadly, not that uncommon, and they come up a lot more the more successful you become. In those cases, your gut is almost always right. I'll give you an example: One of the hardest parts of business is when you have to fire someone. No one likes doing it, but sometimes it's necessary. You're running a business, and when someone on your payroll isn't contributing to that business, there's only so long you can afford to keep them around.

But deciding to let someone go is rarely as simple as looking at a spreadsheet and crunching the numbers. There is a human element involved. When you're running a small business, especially, it's easy for the people you work with to become your friends, or even feel like family. And once you're close to someone like that, it's not just that firing them is hard; it's that making excuses for them is easy.

It becomes all too simple to say, "Oh, he's just been off his game lately," or, "She's been having a tough time at home," or, "Well, he hasn't pulled his weight for a few months now, but he really knocked it out of the park that one time." And it goes on and on. Every time you face the reality that this person just isn't working out anymore, it's tempting to make an excuse on their behalf and let things continue in the hopes that the situation will somehow improve on its own.

Everybody deserves a second chance. Hell, most people deserve a third chance. But there's only so long you can afford to pay someone who isn't doing the job you need them to do. Even someone who works solely on commission—i.e., someone you're not actually paying to be there, someone who's only collecting money if they're producing deals—can still be a drain on your business if they're sitting around the office distracting the other employees all day, or worse, damaging morale by spreading negativity.

At a certain point, you have to say enough is enough.

When one of your workers isn't doing their job, mentally giving them a second chance doesn't help. Giving someone a second chance may feel good, but it only counts if they actually recognize that's what's happening. In other words, you have to actually talk to them and make it clear that they need to shape up, as uncomfortable as that conversation might be. And if that doesn't produce results, you'll quickly find that giving them additional chances has diminishing returns in the "feel-good" department, and even less in terms of productivity.

And while your employee still isn't carrying their weight, you'll be lying awake at night with a sick feeling in the pit of your stomach because your gut is trying to tell you that it's time to make a change, but you're not listening.

Take it from someone who's been there: you can spare yourself, your company, and even your difficult employee a lot of time, stress, and pain if you just face up to what needs to be done and make the difficult cut. It's never fun, but it's ultimately kinder to everyone involved. Your company can move forward, your employee can find something that actually interests them, and most of all, you can breathe easier without this constant stress weighing you down.

Here's a perfect example that happened to me a few years back. I had a trainer at my company whom I'll call Mark. Great guy, great attitude, tons of fun to have around, and he really knew his stuff. Agents loved him and they learned a lot from his training sessions. We'd hang out together when we weren't at the office. I considered him a close personal friend.

After a while, Mark started slacking off in his duties. He'd show up for training sessions late or take off early, leaving new agents who had rearranged their schedules to be there just sitting around with nothing to do. Sometimes he just wouldn't show up at all.

I know what you're thinking: a trainer who doesn't train isn't worth having around. I should have just fired him, or sat him down and given him a specified period to shape up, and then fired him if his performance didn't improve. Well, you're probably right about that. My gut said the same thing. And, for the record, I did sit him down and have that conversation with him about how I needed him to shape up. I had it three or four times, in fact.

Why so many? Well, each time I'd explain the areas in which he'd been slacking off and what I needed to see from him, and each time he'd apologize and promise to do better, and then he'd hit me with a story about how he'd been off his game lately because of one thing or another (or usually a series of things) going wrong in his personal life—rotten stuff, the kind of stuff that makes you really feel for a guy. And like I said, he was a friend. I knew his wife, I knew his family, I knew there were problems behind the scenes. When he told me what was going on, I had no reason to doubt him.

And to be fair, each time I had that conversation with him, he really did turn things around. For a while. Then he'd start flaking on his duties again, even worse than before. And I'd go back to staring at the ceiling at four in the morning wondering if I was paying him and getting nothing in return, and thinking about all the agents who weren't getting a proper training. My gut kept telling me to cut him loose and stop the damage before it got any worse, but my heart kept telling me that would be screwing over a friend who was going through a tough time.

Before I even realized it, a year had gone by like this, a year of wavering back and forth between whether I had to fire Mark or whether I could really trust him to get back on track. Finally, instead of sitting him down and having the same conversation for a fifth time, I put it all in an email to him—*here's what I need you to do, here's how long you have to do it, here's what's going to happen if you don't.* That way, he had my issues and my criteria all in writing, and just as importantly, I had committed myself on paper to delivering real consequences if my conditions (which basically amounted to him doing the job I was paying him to do) weren't met.

Once again, Mark got his act together for a little while. And when he was on, he was on. I had high hopes. But sooner than ever before, he started phoning it in and disappearing again. When I confronted him about it, once again he came at me with stories of all the terrible things that had been going on in his personal life, but I had to stick to my word. I had to terminate him, even knowing that it meant I would lose him as a friend.

Looking back on it now, I regret not listening to my gut about Mark much sooner. I let the fact that he was my friend get in the way of doing what was right for my business. And over the year-plus that I kept him on the company payroll even though he wasn't doing his job, how many agents received poor or incomplete training? A hundred? Two hundred? How many of them struggled to find a foothold in the real estate business because they didn't have the initial training that they were supposed to have? How many quit the business altogether as a result?

I'll never know the exact extent of the impact that had on my business, but I definitely learned my lesson from that experience. I don't regret giving Mark a second chance when he started to slip, or even a third. Even if he wasn't a good friend, or his personal life hadn't been rocky, I would have wanted to give him that much. But letting it go on past that was a mistake, and that mistake—and any consequences from it—were on my head.

At the end of the day, what it comes down to is this: Your heart and your gut can speak to you at the same time. You follow your heart to make yourself feel good, but you follow your gut to prevent yourself from feeling worse.

Combating Negativity

How to handle nasty reviews, complaining coworkers, and the voices in your head

The author Frank Herbert once wrote, "Fear is the mind killer." If that's true, then negativity is the productivity killer. It's toxic to any work environment, and it could even cripple your entire business.

Negativity from Yourself

When you start a new venture, whether it's a career in real estate or in any other business, it may be necessary to put some space between yourself and the most negative people in your life. When people doubt you and constantly question your every move, that incessant negativity can get in your head and make you start doubting yourself. (I'll talk more about how this impacts real estate agents and discuss how to avoid it in Part 3.) For anyone who puts themselves out there, risking their savings and their reputation to build something from scratch, there's a period when letting doubt cripple your instincts and cloud your better judgment can quickly knock you off course and stop you from succeeding before you even get started.

Negativity doesn't just come from the doubters in your personal life, though. It can just as easily come from within, even without someone else's words to set it off. We're all human, we all wrestle with self-doubt, feelings of inadequacy, fear of failure, the whole nine yards. It's only natural for those emotions to surface from time to time, especially when you're taking on a massive challenge like starting your own business, or when you're under a lot of stress.

While you can't always prevent those feelings from cropping up, you can control your response to them. It's easy to let everything that's going wrong in your life—or everything you need to do—overwhelm you. Believe me, I know. But here's my simple, two-step technique for getting past it:

1. **Focus on your goals.** This is one of the reasons why it's so important to have a clear image of your goals in your mind's eye. You need to be able to quickly remind yourself why you're doing this in the first place. Does that goal make you want to work for it? Is it worth a little stress? Can you even imagine someone achieving what you want to achieve without going through some tough times along the way? Take a few minutes to breathe, collect your thoughts, and let your vision of your own better, brighter future inspire you to get up off the mat.

2. **Get something done.** The enemy of procrastination is productivity. Have you ever felt so overwhelmed by everything you have to do that you can't bring yourself to do any of it? Did sitting there worrying about how you're going to get it all done actually accomplish anything, or did it just waste valuable time?

Let me tell you, no matter how rich you get, no matter how successful, no matter how powerful or influential, there is absolutely nothing you can do that will change the fact that there are only twenty-four hours in each day. And I'll tell you something else: sitting there worrying about the size of your to-do list is just about the only 100-percent-guaranteed method of not making it any shorter.

So, when you have a million things to do and a million doubts in your mind, instead of worrying about the best way to tackle it all, just pick something—anything—and go get it done. That feeling of productivity will propel you through the next thing, and the next one, and so on. It might not be the most strategic way of attacking your problems, but any attack is better than none at all, if for no other reason than it will make you feel like your productive self, which is the best version of yourself. It makes you feel like you really can do it. Like the saying goes: Turn your can'ts into cans and your dreams into plans.

It's that simple. Visualize, and go get something done. It's saved my butt more times than I can count. Even with a fantastic team of people behind me, I generally have thirty hours' worth of work to do in any twenty-four-hour period, and that's assuming that everything is running smoothly. And on top of that, I have a family who occasionally likes to see me, and every now and then, just for the novelty of it, I like to get a few hours of sleep.

My point is this: every single day in my life has the potential to overwhelm me. And as far as I've come, as much as I've accomplished, I'm still susceptible to moments of doubt and panic. But now when those moments occur, I just visualize my goals, I pick something to tackle, and I just blow right past them.

Negativity from Your Coworkers

Negativity can also come from the people you work with. More often than not, it's not someone directly attacking you and your capabilities. While that sort of direct attack certainly can happen, that's generally an HR problem, and it's something a good company tries to snuff out.

The kind of negativity you need to watch out for when it comes to your coworkers is much more insidious than that, because it can often seem like just the background noise of the workplace. I call them **doubtcasters**—people who project negativity around them so consistently that it can drag a whole office down.

Doubtcasters can be people who sit around the office all day complaining about how things aren't going their way. They're not looking for guidance or solutions, they're not looking for someone to help them shore up their weaknesses, they're just looking for people to tell them it's not their fault and agree with them that the world is unfair. They want everyone around them to be as miserable and unproductive as they are, so they won't feel so bad about themselves by comparison (FYI, when you're in a slump, you have to stay positive to keep from turning into this kind of doubtcaster yourself).

Doubtcasters can be people who want to take up the time of other people in the office talking about what's wrong with the company. No company is perfect. No company has ever been perfect, and no company will ever be perfect. Constructive suggestions for how a company can improve should always be welcome. Some of the best ideas for streamlining processes at Rapid Realty came from agents who were out there in the thick of it, handling deals every day long after my daily grind had shifted away from working directly with clients. But people offering solutions are very different from doubtcasters who just want to talk about how things don't work exactly the way they feel they ought to. All the doubtcasters are looking for is an audience that will confirm what they already believe everyone should know—that they're the smartest person in the room, and everyone should be taking orders from them.

And then there are the doubtcasters who spend their days complaining about the state of the industry as an excuse for their lack of success. They point their fingers at the state of the market and say, "No one could make money in conditions like this," all while making no actual attempt to make money whatsoever. Don't get me wrong, some industries are legitimately volatile. Sometimes markets really do plummet and demand for a particular good or service dries up. If you were a mortgage broker in 2008, you had a genuine complaint about the state of your industry. If you work for a company that makes VCRs, you have a legitimate beef. But I remember during 2007–2009, perhaps the biggest boom years the apartment rental industry had ever seen, when I'd still come into the office and hear one or two rental agents complaining about how it was impossible to close a deal in that market. Meanwhile, other agents sitting two desks over were making money like they'd never seen before.

The problem with doubtcasters is not just that they're unproductive, although it's never great to have someone sitting around your company all day not producing anything, even if they're working solely on commission. The real problem is that they're toxic to morale. It's extremely difficult to be within earshot of that constant stream of negativity without being affected by it. It takes an iron will to stop all those complaints from taking root in your brain and sprouting into doubts of your own.

When you spend time around doubtcasters, it's almost inevitable that you will start to wonder, "Wow, is there really something fundamentally wrong with this company? Is there really something fundamentally impossible about this industry? Is there really something fundamentally unfair about the world?" If you're a philosopher, by all means, go nuts on those questions. But if you're operating a business and you're trying to achieve your financial goals, then parking yourself on a chair and spending hours wondering if the world is against you will achieve precisely zero.

That's why you need to put some distance between yourself and any doubtcasters in your office. If they're your employees, for the good of your whole office, you need to take them aside and have a conversation about their attitude and their future as a part of your team. And if they don't report to you, or if they outrank you, and there's really no one you can speak to about this toxic presence in the office, just do whatever you can to block them out. Don't let their commitment to accomplishing nothing drag you down too. Throw on some noise-cancelling headphones, stop hanging out in the break room, move to a different part of the office—whatever you need to do.

Get as far away from your office's doubtcasters as you can. And then go out there and prove them wrong by doing your job and doing it well. Misery loves company; that's why doubtcasters want you to be miserable too. If you show them that you love what you do and you're determined to be great at it, they'll find someone else to bore. You might even be the inspiration they need to remember why they got into this job in the first place.

Negativity from Your Clients

We live in an age when everyone carries a megaphone in their pocket. With so many online review sites and services, it doesn't take much for someone to hop online and let the world know what they think of you and your business. For a company that's just getting off the ground, positive reviews can be vital for attracting a customer base, but just a small handful of negative reviews can have real and immediate consequences.

Managing your online reputation is critically important these days, but it's not always easy, and the odds can be stacked against you. Review sites all have their own rules for what can and cannot be posted, and whether or not a business can respond. On their surface, one thing all of these sites share is that they are committed, first and foremost, to objectivity. That is, they have a vested interest in ensuring that anyone who posts a glowing review of a business really is a satisfied customer and not an employee in disguise, and that anyone who posts a terrible review is really a customer who had a bad experience rather than a competitor, disgruntled former employee looking for revenge, or just someone trolling the business for the fun of it.

The trouble, of course, is that there's no way a popular review site could possibly fact-check each individual review by hand. It would be completely impossible to verify each and every experience. So each site has its own carefully guarded method of automatically filtering reviews to weed out the ones that seem suspicious. And a computer algorithm tasked with the job of checking opinion-based statements posted by human beings with an infinite range of different backgrounds, language skills, and ways of expressing themselves is guaranteed to make mistakes. Real reviews get taken down, fake reviews are left up. It's unfortunate, but it's the nature of the beast.

This is a subject I sadly know all too well. Earlier in this book, I talked a bit about the turmoil that Rapid Realty went through back around 2007, when several top agents suddenly left the company to start competing firms, poached a bunch of other agents away to work for them, and then started a concentrated campaign to smear Rapid Realty by posting fraudulent reviews online posing as dissatisfied clients. They made all kinds of false, outlandish claims about our agents behaving in horrible and unprofessional ways, accused us of harassing and scamming our clients, and made us out to be an almost cartoonishly terrible company. Because these false reviews were being planted by former Rapid Realty agents, they knew enough about the company to insert just enough truth into their reviews that they often seemed just plausible enough to avoid being taken off the sites immediately.

That was one of the most difficult periods I've ever gone through in my life. First, there was the betrayal that I felt, knowing that these malicious false reviews were being planted by people I had personally trained, worked with, and had once considered friends. But on top of that, even though they were flagrant lies, all these phony reviews were having a measurable impact on my

business—they were actually making it harder for me and the people I worked with to achieve our dreams.

I felt like I was taking crazy pills every day. I knew that these reviews were all lies, but the rest of the world thought they were true. It's a fundamental fact of life that if someone accuses you of something you didn't do, the louder you protest, the more people will think it's really true. So even when these reviews were posted on sites that allowed us to respond, posting a reply just often made things worse. It honestly felt like waking up one day and everyone around you suddenly insisting that the sky is orange.

Ultimately, we were able to prove that a good number of these reviews were false, and had been planted by our competitors or people hired by our competitors. In some cases, we were able to disprove the reviews by catching them in a lie; in other cases we were able to provide evidence that our competitors had conspired to put these reviews out there. But we couldn't get rid of them all, and even if we could have, they had already done significant damage. Those reviews were up on the internet for long enough to color the perception of our company in the public eye for years.

In the end, we took a long, hard look at our company and came to the conclusion that maybe there was a reason these reviews were able to take root in the court of public opinion. Even though the precise experiences recounted in these reviews were totally made up, the fact that anyone thought they could be real meant they were willing to believe the worst about us (granted, people love to think that companies are evil, and a fair number of people are biased against real estate companies to begin with). We actually released a statement in the press apologizing for any poor customer service we might have delivered in the past and announcing our commitment to doing better for all our clients. One deal at a time, we reearned the trust that had been stolen from us. And of course, Rapid Realty recovered and went on to become bigger and better than ever. But that wasn't the end of our trouble with online reviews.

See, review sites claim to prize objectivity above everything

else, but at the end of the day, they're businesses like any other. They're not perfect, and they're not immune to greed. The review service Yelp once gave Rapid Realty an award in recognition of how many positive reviews we had received. Then they asked us if we would like to start paying a monthly fee for access to some extra services. We declined, since we'd been doing just fine getting positive feedback without those services—we'd won their award, after all! Almost immediately, the vast majority of those positive reviews disappeared.

Naturally, Yelp claimed that their algorithm had just coincidentally filtered out all those reviews under suspicion that they might be fraudulent—and mind you, in some cases, these were reviews that grateful clients had written right in front of my eyes, or had sent me a copy of in an email—and that they "might" come back one day, after their algorithm received another round of fine-tuning.

Yelp has actually been on the receiving end of numerous lawsuits from other companies that have precisely the same story of extortion. As of this writing, none of those lawsuits have been successful, largely because Yelp is so secretive about their algorithm that it is virtually impossible to prove any wrongdoing. But it's worth noting that after a very close call in court, Yelp changed the language on their site to no longer say that their algorithm "filters" reviews. It now says that it "recommends or does not recommend" reviews. So if your review doesn't appear on the site, it's not because they took it down to control the reputation of a company that wouldn't pay them for services it didn't want; it's because it's simply "not recommended at this time."

OK, I know, I sound bitter. And when it comes to this subject, maybe I am. But I'm bitter because I've been through the ringer when it comes to online reviews. I've been on the receiving end of every dirty trick in the book. With any luck at all, you'll never have to deal with a smear campaign or a site trying to extort you out of your money. But even so, negative reviews are a fact of life now. So,

please, learn from my example and let me give you a few pointers for how to handle negative reviews for your own business.

Don't respond to every negative comment. If someone raises a legitimate concern, and the site allows you to respond, by all means post a response. But keep it short and respectful, and always remember that you're representing your business. Even if the customer is being completely unreasonable, getting into a verbal fight with them won't make your business look good. It will look like a big, bad company is ganging up on the little guy. And don't feel like you have to respond to every single thing that's out there about your company. First of all, you'll never keep up with the volume, and you'll drive yourself crazy trying. And second, you'll come across as desperate, and nobody likes desperation.

Understand that people are entitled to their opinions. Even Superman has people who think he's a weirdo for wearing his underwear outside his pants. You need a thick skin to be an entrepreneur. People can be ruthless on the internet, but just let them vent and move on. Save your time and energy for proving the facts, not debating opinions.

Know your rights. If you see a negative review that you believe to be false, or misleading, take a long look at the site's terms of service. Most review sites have strict codes about what kind of claims reviewers can and cannot make about a business. If a review crosses the line, it's generally not terribly difficult to have it removed. Most sites really are interested in maintaining some community standards.

Control who responds. You don't need every person in your company posting responses to negative comments. It should be the job of one or two people. When it becomes a free-for-all, it's far too easy for someone to lose their cool. And as soon as one of your employees loses their temper and starts flinging mud online,

that's all people will want to talk about. That one employee, who may have been acting without any authority from you or your company, can still do far more damage to the reputation of your business than the original negative review.

Fight negativity with positivity. When responding to a negative comment, thank the writer for their feedback and tell them you'd love to work with them again so they can see that you've taken their comments to heart. People respond well to a company that can admit its mistakes and wants to do better. A customer who had a poor experience on one visit may amend or delete their negative remarks if they have a better experience the next time around. And of course, the best way to combat negative reviews is with a flood of positive reviews, so encourage everyone at your company to go out there and earn them!

Building Your Empire and Sharing the Load

Good help may be hard to find, but the
search can change your life

It's been said many times before: no one succeeds alone. As much as that might be a cliché, it was still one of the toughest lessons for me to take to heart, and I know a lot of other entrepreneurs who feel the same way. When you create a business from the ground up, there's often a long period where you do everything yourself because:

A. The scale of your business is small enough that you can realistically oversee it all.

B. It's your vision, and you want it executed your way.

But as your business grows, you will eventually reach a point where running the whole show yourself becomes impossible; there are just too many moving parts. Many entrepreneurs go through a period when they burn the candle at both ends, foregoing sleep, ignoring personal relationships, and rejecting any well-intentioned offers of help, before they finally admit that they need someone to share the workload. I know I certainly did.

If you're lucky, wise, or an extremely fortunate combination of both, you'll reach that realization before it affects your work. It's very easy to give yourself all kinds of excuses for inconsistent quality in your work, especially when you're running on fumes. You can fall into the trap of telling yourself that your new client won't mind if your service is spotty; they'll somehow know that you gave great service to the five clients who came before them, and they'll cut you some slack. But the truth is, your clients and customers don't care how exhausted you are, or how many balls you have in the air. They don't see themselves as a part of your story; they see you as a small part of theirs. That's why consistency is so important.

As your business grows and the demands on your time multiply, the only way to maintain consistent service for your customers—and often consistent management for your employees—is to bite the bullet and delegate. There are two ways to do this: expanding your staff, or taking on a partner.

Expanding Your Team

What's the difference between a boss and a leader? A boss says, "Go." A leader says, "Let's go." A boss has people who work under him, but a leader has a team.

If you're going to make a career as an entrepreneur, you'll need a team. These team members won't be just your employees or your partners, they'll be people you work with in one way or another, and it's best to regard them as part of your business family, rather than merely allies, or resources. Your team might include inspectors, designers, lawyers, accountants, publicists, contractors, subcontractors, tax professionals, credit professionals, insurance professionals, and lenders, just to name a few.

Many of these jobs can be done by outside parties. You might hire an outside accounting firm to keep your business's books, for instance. But as your organization grows in size and complexity, you will inevitably have to hand off the reins to some of the daily internal operations to people you trust.

For me, appointing Carlos Angelucci as Rapid Realty's chief operating officer was a massive act of delegation, and a huge leap of trust. It wasn't the first time I'd given some measure of control to someone else at Rapid; I had appointed trainers and put people in managerial or administrative positions before. Hell, it wasn't even the first time I'd put Carlos in a position of authority; I'd trusted him with training and recruiting agents for the whole company. But by making him COO, I gave him decision-making power over basically all the day-to-day details that kept the company running. He was my voice when I couldn't be there in person, and I trusted his judgment enough to let him handle those details when I needed to be focusing on the bigger picture.

It wasn't easy to let the small things go, at least at first. That's not an attack on Carlos—by the time I gave him the COO position, I knew he'd do a fantastic job with it—it's just that, as an entrepreneur, you start out doing, well, whatever it is your company does: renting apartments, designing posters, making widgets. Then you take on employees and become a manager, and you get used to doing that instead. Then you delegate the daily managerial tasks so you can focus on the direction your company is moving, and you have to get used to doing that. There are adjustments at every step, and every step requires trust.

Turning Rapid Realty into a franchise was also a massive exercise in trusting people. The number one reason I was initially resistant to the idea of franchising was that it would limit the amount of direct control I would have on each of the offices. I would have to trust each franchisee with representing the brand I had created in the manner I hoped it would be represented, and I had to trust that they would hire people who would represent their offices the same way. If there was a broken link in that chain, being

a franchisor instead of an owner would limit the amount I could intervene. Taking that leap of faith was difficult, but it was one of the best decisions I ever made.

Delegating is also about having the self-awareness to recognize your own weaknesses and your team members' strengths. Carlos and I used to design recruiting ads ourselves. Then we started routinely needing more advanced graphic design work done than we could do ourselves, so we hired a media director. We used to write all the company manuals and memos ourselves; then we reached a point where we simply didn't have the time to devote to writing them, and we certainly didn't have the time to devote to rewriting them, so we hired a communications director. And on and on. These were all hires from within, tapping the talents and trained skills of our people and letting them do what they do best.

Whenever you delegate by creating positions like this, you have to take the time to clearly define the role. With franchisees, that definition is laid out in a legally binding contract, so that tends to make things nice and clear. But whether you're handing off a task to an outside contractor or creating a new position for someone inside your organization, it's important to establish the purpose of this role and the limits of their authority and autonomy.

- What are the goals of this position? What problems will it solve, or at least take off your hands?
- What responsibilities will this position have in order to be useful and distinct from the other roles your company already has?
- Can the person in this position spend your company's money?
- If so, will they have discretion over a separate budget, or do all purchases need to be approved by someone higher up?
- Can they enforce company policy? That is, if they see a company rule being broken, can they step in and address the situation?

- If they can enforce policy, can they create it?
- What parts of their job can they do without getting your approval (or the approval of another ranking person in your company)?
- What parts of their job *always* require your approval?

Even with the answers to all these questions firmly established, delegating responsibilities like this is not an instant fix. Even if you're tapping someone from within your organization, when you promote them and give them a new level of responsibilities, it's like hiring someone new. There's going to be a period where you have to train them, or where you have to look over their shoulder and make sure that what they're doing is what you really need. But if you choose your help wisely and trust people to do their jobs, you'll quickly find yourself changing from the owner of a company into its leader.

Choosing a Partner

Sometimes delegating responsibilities isn't enough. Sometimes the best way to keep your company going is to make another person a full partner in your enterprise—sharing the profits and sharing the expenses. The right partner can boost your business to new heights; the wrong one can be its downfall. Here are some questions to consider before you commit to a partner:

Do you really need a partner, or would you prefer an employee? If you need to bring someone into your company to take care of certain tasks—if you want someone to come in every morning, do a good job on the tasks you set for him, and go home at quitting time—it's almost always best to find a good worker and pay him a salary, rather than giving him a direct interest in the business. Take a partner if you need someone to both put capital into the business and add value to the business.

What are your objectives in taking on a partner? You probably need a partner to bring something to the business that you lack. If all you need is capital, you can usually raise it without allowing someone into your business who'll have a direct say in its operations. A partner should be someone who can bring a skill or a service to the table that you don't have yourself.

For example, are you a great thinker but poor at interpersonal skills? Then you might want to bring in an extroverted person who's good at sales and networking. If you're a big-picture person, your partner might be someone who can control the budget and see to the details. A partner should *not* be someone who does the same thing you do.

What are the prospective partner's objectives in working with you? What does he or she bring to the business that you lack? What kind of a return is expected? How much time, money, and elbow grease is this prospective partner willing to commit to the business? If you have a gut feeling that a potential partner is making untenable promises, trust your gut. Look for a partner who tells you up front what his or her limits are.

Is the prospect forthcoming about finances? It's not pleasant to have to do this kind of due diligence on another person, but you've got to find out where your partner's financial commitments lie, whether your partner really can deliver the capital promised, and whether your partner will be able to live on the limited returns your business is likely to realize in the first year or two. If you're counting on a substantial financial commitment from someone, investigate finances as though you were a bank making a home loan. If your partner resists this type of scrutiny, it's probably not a good risk. And be prepared to disclose your finances as well—a smart partner will want to do the same due diligence on you.

Does the prospect share your vision and enthusiasm? The two of you don't have to agree on everything, but your basic ideas for the direction of the business should mesh—and your partner should

be eager not just to start a business, but to start a business *with you*. If that enthusiasm doesn't stay strong, a lackadaisical attitude will get communicated to your employees and clients, and that will hurt the team.

What's the word on the street about this prospect? It's a salesman's business to be charming, and your prospective partner is selling that personality to you. That's fine, but don't let yourself be snowed.

Ask around. Does this person pay debts? How does this person act under pressure? How has this person handled failures? It's not necessary that your prospect be generally liked, but this person must be trustable.

Talk to people who have worked for your prospect, and to former employers. Find out how he or she treats people he or she doesn't have to be nice to.

Does the prospect ask the right questions? Does your prospect do as much due diligence on you? Does your prospect challenge your ideas? If it seems to you that this person is not curious enough, you might be dealing with a hasty person, who makes decisions based on insufficient information and then has second thoughts.

Will the prospect sign a contract? Will you? Lots of people boast that their word and their handshake are absolute guarantees. And many people, in many walks of life, do business on a word and a handshake. Sometimes that's all you need. A full partnership in a business, though, usually requires a written contract. For one thing, if the terms are written down in black and white, you'll sometimes spot potential problems in the agreement, and work them out before you sign. You might find contingencies that will have to be addressed in writing. You might find disagreements that you didn't know you had, which will have to be ironed out before you can finalize the partnership.

A written contract is also an important part of your exit strategy, which you have to have. What if a crisis comes up, and one

of you isn't able to fulfill his part of the agreement? What if one of you totally flakes out? What if you just plain can't work together? All of these issues will have to be addressed in the contract.

And get a lawyer to draw it up. Contracts written by amateurs are usually recipes for disaster.

How to Avoid Failure

Lots of people dream of an entrepreneurial career in which they're wildly successful, can retire early, and can spend the rest of their lives being looked up to by other aspiring young people. Only a few of them go that far, though. More often than not, they'll hit a level of success that falls far below their expectations, and then spend years just trying to stay afloat. Some would-be entrepreneurs fail utterly, go broke, and give up—and end up with a 9-to-5 job just as they'd dreaded all along. And a lot of people dream, but never actually try to realize the dream.

Entrepreneurs fail for many different reasons. Let me tell you what some of the main ones are, so you'll have a better chance of avoiding them.

Being Too Protective of Your Initial Gains. Many people have a little success when they start out in a business, and immediately start to worry about losing that initial gain. Money isn't worth anything if you hoard it. Once you've met your expenses, you've got to sink your leftover assets into your business. Sometimes you'll make mistakes; sometimes forces outside your control will work against you—and sometimes you'll take a loss as a result. But you have to be willing to take that risk. Believe me on this: If you're careful, and responsible, and put in the effort, the risk to your capital will be a lot smaller than you might think.

Listening to the Naysayers. People who have low tolerance for risk will advise you not to start your own business but to get a regular job instead, or get a postgraduate degree in something "useful." Or

they might just tell you, "You'll never make it in business: you're not the type." If someone can give you a clear, well-reasoned argument as to why your ideas won't work, you might want to pay them some attention. But if all they can give you is a generalized, "I wouldn't if I were you," then probably your best policy is just to say, "No, you wouldn't."

Hubris. Conversely, a lot of entrepreneurs have unrealistic opinions about their own competence, intelligence, and capabilities. They might believe that they can do a difficult thing without first learning how, or they might think they can handle a huge project without help. Ambition is good, risk taking is good—but only if you understand what you can do and what you'll need to do it.

You can't be too proud to admit that there's more you need to learn. When I decided to get into franchising, if I had just leapt in and assumed I'd knock it out of the park, it would have been a disaster. But because I spent a year learning as much as I could about franchising first, I was able to expand my company quickly at a time when most companies were downsizing.

Likewise, getting over your pride and realizing where you have weaknesses is key to making smart hiring or partnership decisions. It wasn't until I came to terms with my own limitations that I finally hired an assistant to take some things off my plate. And that first act of delegating made it easier to do it again when the time came to hire strategists, a communications and PR team, and of course, a COO—all necessary elements for the growth of my company and brand, and all choices I made because I was able to put my pride aside and recognize where I needed help.

Giving Up Too Soon. Believe me, even the most confident people in the world get frustrated sometimes. They fail, or they come up short of their own expectations, and they want to just say "To hell with it," and walk away from the whole enterprise. I've wanted to just quit, more than once. But I'd advise you, when the situation looks hopeless, to remember the words of Sir Winston Churchill:

"Never give in, never give in, never, never, never—in nothing, great or small, large or petty. Never give in except to convictions of honor and good sense. Never yield to force; never yield to the apparently overwhelming might of the enemy."

Sure, you'll question your own abilities. You'll question whether or not you're on the right course. You'll question whether your goal, and your chance of achieving it, are worth the effort. You're human, so you'll have self-doubts and you'll want to walk away.

Instead of walking away, instead of losing hope—and instead of making the same mistake over and over and expecting a different result—figure out what you've been doing wrong, or how to avoid the traps you've fallen into. Reassess, readjust, regroup—and resist the urge to quit.

I thought about calling it quits after I lost a building in a fire and one of my tenants died. I thought about throwing in the towel after my dad died and my top brokers betrayed me right as I was about to entrust them with the growth of my company. But each time I was on the verge of being wiped out financially, emotionally, or both, I refocused on why I was doing this in the first place— what I wanted to achieve for myself and my family—and it gave me the strength to pick myself up off the mat and go harder than ever. And that's why I'm where I am today.

Just remember, in every story that's worth telling, the hero has to overcome obstacles to get what they want. And the bigger the obstacles, the more satisfying it is when they come out on top in the end. Your life is your story, so be the hero.

Going It Alone. I've read that one of the most common reasons why a business fails is that it's a one-man operation. I'm a self-starter, a self-motivator, and a lot of what I've accomplished has been on my own initiative—but I've always known that I need other people to help me go places.

You need to know intelligent, informed people who will challenge your ideas, give you advice, and maybe even invest their money and their know-how.

You need to know hardworking people, because eventually you'll want them working for you or with you.

You need to know people with money. They might want to invest in your enterprise, and even if they don't, they might know someone who would.

You need to know people with connections, who can introduce you to other people who can help you accomplish your goals.

It's easy to build effective networks, even if you're a shy person who keeps to yourself, and I'll discuss how to do it later in this book. But you've got to do it. Time and again, you'll have to ask people for help, and you'll want to invite people to work with you. When the time comes, you've got to know the right people.

Not Knowing Why People Should Work with You. You know how many rental brokers there are in New York City? Neither do I, but it's a lot. If you want to rent an apartment, or if you have an apartment to rent, there are plenty of offices you can visit. If I'm going to convince you to come to my office, I have to be able to explain to myself why you would want to. It's the same in any business, whether you're selling snake oil, developing properties, or managing a mutual fund: You have to know why people would want to buy your snake oil, let you develop their land, or let you manage their money. And you have to be able communicate that reason to someone else, and do it in a way that will keep their interest. That's where a good elevator pitch comes in handy. (See Part 3 to learn how to craft a good elevator pitch.)

Lack of Capital. Sure, you hear rags-to-riches stories of the guy who started a business without even the price of a pack of gum in his pocket, and became a gazillionaire. Well, those are stories. Something like that has happened here and there, maybe, but in the real world you have to spend money to make money. Profitability never happens overnight, and there are a thousand examples of businesses that ran out of runway right when they were *this close* to taking off. Be sure you have enough capital to get

you through those tough early times—because they will be tough, and expensive.

• • •

Thomas Edison once said that opportunity shows up in overalls and looks like work. That's why a lot of people don't recognize it.

Being a public figure means being on stage and making the world forget that there's anything behind the curtain. Intellectually, of course, everyone knows that there's a lot going on behind me that they can't see—but people like to pretend that what they're seeing is all there is. People love illusions; they're entertained and inspired by illusions. A successful illusion must seem to have been created without effort—and it must be flawless. It must never contain even the slightest hint that it is an illusion.

But the one person I can never fool is myself—and that'll go for you, too, if you set out on an entrepreneurial career. The more successful you are, the more you'll be reminded of the countless hours, days, weeks, months, and years of hard work that have happened, and are still happening, behind the curtain.

I started out in real estate with simple aspirations: to work hard and make money. I wanted to give back to my parents in such a way that they would never have to worry about finances.

Pretty early on I realized that real estate was a great match for my personality and work style. I liked the freedom I had to set my own schedule and plan my own day. I also liked the commissions!

My mother encouraged me to go beyond the level of an agent and to open my own real estate office. So, I did. I put a lot of hours into building my business, and I still do. I did whatever it took to keep moving forward and to make a profit.

I also went on to open up a real estate school and a construction business, among many other businesses. I'm making my dreams come true with "sweat equity"—and with a smile. I started with almost nothing and I'm very proud of what I've achieved.

For aspiring entrepreneurs, or for anyone working their way

up from the bottom, my story is proof that just about any dream is achievable, given dedication and hard work. My result is born from an imperfect situation—just as yours will be—and best of all, my story affirms that the American Dream is alive and well.

Stress Management

As the old saying goes, if you don't love what you're doing, why do it? It's a good line, but it ignores an essential truth: no one loves everything about their job every day. I don't care if you're a real estate agent, a rock star, or a professional puppy petter, no matter how wonderful and rewarding your career is, at some point—probably multiple points—it's going to create some major stress in your life (although if you've managed to earn a living petting puppies, honestly, no one wants to hear you complain).

Success doesn't come easy. But just because you're going to encounter some stress along the way doesn't mean you have to let it rule your life. When you're feeling overwhelmed, like life just doesn't want you to succeed, here are a few tips to help you push past it and get back to loving what you do.

Remember the Odds. No one knocks it out of the park every time they step up to the plate. But no one strikes out every time either. When you're having trouble getting a deal to come together, take a minute to think about your past transactions. Think about the ones where you came out on top, and what you did right. Think about the ones that fell through and what you learned. Think about the ones that looked like they were going to crumble, and then worked out at the last minute.

And if that doesn't help you get in the right mindset, think back to other times you beat the odds. Me, I like to think about my childhood. I think of where I started and how little we had, about all the doors that got slammed in my face when I was starting out in business, and then I look around and see where I am today. If

I could get from there to here, I've already beaten the odds. One little deal is nothing compared to that.

Make Some Progress—Any Progress. When the size of your to-do list gets you so stressed out that you feel like you're too paralyzed to do anything, just pick a task and get to work. It doesn't have to be the most strategically brilliant choice, it doesn't have to be the absolute smartest, most efficient place to begin, just pick something and do it. Even if it means breaking up the tasks on your to-do list into smaller tasks, making your list even longer, just so you can knock one of them out, that's okay. Find a way to cross something off that list, no matter how small it is. Stress may be paralyzing, but productivity is addictive. Once you get a taste of that great feeling of productivity, you'll want more. If you can keep that momentum going, you'll be amazed by what you can accomplish.

Be Honest and Claim Responsibility. If you screw up, own up. Every so often, you're going to drop the ball. And knowing that you dropped it is one of the worst stress creators. If you didn't get an applicant's papers in on time, or you misplaced a key, own up, take responsibility, and be honest. Clients, coworkers, and your company will respect you more for being a person of integrity and you'll feel much better being honest than you would have if you'd masked the problem. Also, if you make a mistake and then make up for it to the best of your ability, people will remember that you apologized and tried to make amends—and that will count more with them than the mistake.

Exercise. Running around the city can seem like a workout in itself, but make sure you dedicate some time each day—or at least three times a week—to a serious workout, even if it's just a long walk outdoors. The endorphins your brain releases during a workout can help improve your mood and relieve stress. You'll come back to your work with a clearer and happier perspective.

I'll be honest with you: there have been a lot of times in my

life when I've struggled with this particular piece of advice. When I built my mansion, I included a pool and a great home gym, and I still went through long periods where I didn't use any of it. I'd tell myself it was because I was too busy working—and I was—but no matter how much energy you're burning every day for work, it's not the same as an honest workout, either for your physical or your mental health. But the times when I've been the happiest, regardless of what was going on in my career, have been the times when I've committed to exercising regularly.

In fact, while I was writing this book, I made the most con-certed effort I've ever made in exercising. I even hired a trainer to make sure I didn't slack off. The period when I was working on this book was possibly the busiest in my life—Rapid Realty was expanding to new territories that had me traveling all over the country, I was expanding my business holdings in new directions beyond anything I'd done before, I was buying and selling multiple properties simultaneously, I was overseeing multiple construction and development projects, and to top it all off, I had a newborn baby at home. I had more things going on that could potentially stress me out than ever before, and yet I've never been happier or felt more ready to take it all on. That's the power of exercise.

Remind Yourself that This, Too, Shall Pass. People often find themselves in situations that feel as though they'll never end. It's a psychological phenomenon—people are programmed to think that whatever's happening now will continue happening indefinitely. That's why gamblers think their hot streak will never end, and it's why, when you hit a slump, it feels like you'll never be able to shake it. Whether it's a personal issue or a lousy market, it's easy to feel like the dark clouds will never part. But the truth is, they always do. Look at the recession—the worst economic disaster most of us will ever see (with a little luck, that is). In 2008, it felt like things were so bad, it would be amazing if any business could ever turn a profit again. The entire American way of life seemed as if it were dangling on the precipice. But you know what? We bounced back.

No matter the scale, all things eventually pass. In the worst-case scenario, as a last resort, you can use your talent and know-how in another location where the market is more attractive.

Remember to Have Fun. If you've ever said "I don't deserve a night off," this one's for you. Stress comes with any job, and sometimes the best way to deal with it is to blow off some steam. It's only natural to feel like you need to be working 24/7 when you have a to-do list that's growing longer before your eyes. But everybody needs—and just as importantly, *deserves*—some balance.

Give yourself a break every now and again. Go see a movie, have a night on the town, spend the weekend with friends or with someone you love. People need a little relaxation and a change of pace to recharge their batteries. It's healthy, and it will help you be more productive when you go back to work.

Some of my favorite memories of Rapid Realty are our company ski trips. There we'd be, up in the mountains—franchisees who had been working like they'd never worked before to build successful small businesses for themselves, executives like me who had been burning the candle at both ends overseeing a swiftly growing brand, and agents new and old, some who had been making more money than they'd ever seen in their lives, and others who had been struggling to close a deal. Up there on the slopes, none of that mattered. We could all just have fun and enjoy one another's company. And even if we never talked shop for a minute, when we came back to the city, back to reality, everyone would go back to work with just as much enthusiasm and determination as if they'd been at a weeklong training seminar.

Remember Your Community. Stress makes you feel lousy about yourself. But you know what's a surefire cure for that? Helping your community. You don't need to hand out giant checks to do some good. Spend an hour before or after work helping out at your local food pantry or homeless shelter. Organize a canned food drive in your office to help the needy, or collect school supplies or toys for underprivileged kids. Go to your closest animal shelter and ask if they need help walking the dogs. Opportunities to do some good are all around you, and they don't come with a price tag.

I'm immensely proud of how much Rapid Realty has grown since I started it back in 1998, and of all the good it's able to do with so many offices and agents. We've participated in Habitat for Humanity builds, organized benefit shows for the American Cancer Society, and come together in myriad ways to support some wonderful organizations. But when I think about the moment as CEO of Rapid Realty when I felt most strongly that this company I created was truly capable of doing some good, the moment that comes to mind was actually long before we started franchising, back when the entire company was just a couple dozen people.

On the night before Thanksgiving, we'd all pile into a couple of vans and split up, heading all over Brooklyn. We'd ninja our way into apartment buildings (if there's one thing real estate agents know how to do, it's get into buildings) and knock on the doors of disadvantaged families. When they answered, they'd find us waiting in the halls with baskets filled with everything they could possibly need for a bountiful Thanksgiving feast—turkeys, cranberry sauce, stuffing, gravy, the works. Sometimes it was a single parent who would answer the door; sometimes the whole family would be there, including young kids. Seeing the way they'd light up, knowing that they were going to be able to celebrate Thanksgiving the way it's meant to be celebrated—that feeling of making a real, immediate difference in someone's life and doing it as a team— that's something that warms my heart even now.

November and December are traditionally tough months for real estate agents. Everyone who wanted to move before the start of the school year has already moved, and no one likes going apartment hunting in the cold. As I said in Part 1, the first agent to get a Rapid Realty tattoo did it to keep himself focused and motivated during his first winter as an agent. But the way everyone's spirits would be up around the office after those nights of handing out Thanksgiving feasts, the way everyone would cheer each other on

and dive into their work, you'd think it was the best season of the year.

So when stress has got you down, carve out some time to do something to help someone less fortunate. You'll be doing good, and you feel good, and when you feel good, nothing can stop you.

PART 3

Becoming a Broker

First things first, let's quickly discuss terminology. When people talk about a real estate agent, they're generally talking about someone with a salesperson's license, which is the entry-level license in the world of real estate rentals or sales. Someone with a salesperson's license can't open their own real estate office or oversee real estate transactions on their own; their license must be associated with a broker.

The exact definition and requirements for a broker's license vary from state to state, but in general we're talking about a more advanced license that allows you to take on greater responsibility. In New York, for example, you need to pass an exam to get a salesperson's license, and then you have to work as a salesperson in good standing for at least two years and pass another, much more challenging exam to qualify for a broker's license.

As a broker, you can start your own firm, open multiple offices, and have any number of agents working under you. But under the law, any mistakes your agents make can fall on your head.

Even people in the media who write about real estate for a living often use the terms *broker* and *agent* interchangeably, but it's important to appreciate the difference. If you're just starting out in real estate, you're most likely going to be getting your salesperson's license, and that means you're going to be paying your dues and working under someone else for a while. Most agents never become brokers, but every broker used to be an agent. So, if your dream is to own your own business, then step one is to read up on

the rules in your state so that you know exactly what you have to do to make the leap from agent to broker—from employee to boss.

Fighting Negativity

Why you need to be positive—and get
away from your haters

You'll never succeed. You're not cut out for this. This line of work is too damn risky, and you don't have what it takes to stick with it. You'd have to be stupid to want to work in real estate. You'd be better off working as a temp; at least then you might develop some useful skills.

How do you feel after reading that? Pretty motivated, right? No? You mean you don't find it inspiring when people insult you and your choices and tell you you're destined for failure? Imagine that!

Unfortunately, when you make the decision to get into real estate, you're likely to hear criticism just like that. And the worst part is, it will likely come from the people closest to you. They'll mean well, they'll think they're just looking out for you, but the fact of the matter is, when you're first starting out, your friends and family can be your biggest doubters.

It makes sense when you think about it—of course the people closest to you would be the ones who would try to talk you out of starting a career in real estate. Who else would care enough to worry like that?

If there's one thing I wish for you, even more than for you to become rich and successful, it's for you to be surrounded by people who love and care about you. What greater measure of a good life could there be? So, sure, when you tell your loved ones that you're planning to get into real estate and they initially express some doubts, accept their comments for what they are—expressions of concern for you and your future. Be prepared to tell them what you hope to get out of real estate and how you plan to get it. (This is one of the reasons why it's important to have a clear picture of success in your mind right from the start.) Hopefully, they'll listen to your reasoning, see your point of view, and offer their support. But there may be some people who refuse to support you. And in the worst cases, you need to be prepared to put some distance between yourself and them for a little while.

It's not hard to see why some people would be suspicious of a career in real estate and want to deter you from going down that path. People are conditioned from an early age to think that a 9-to-5 job is normal, even if it makes you miserable, and that any other kind of work schedule is strange; that the security of a salaried position is worth far more than the unpredictability of a commission-based business; that real estate is a feast-or-famine business and the feast can't possibly outweigh the famine; and that salespeople are sleazy and cutthroat by nature.

In a lot of cases, those criticisms all stem from a single fact: they can't picture themselves doing real estate, so they can't imagine why you'd want to do it either. But think about it: people are different in every other aspect of their lives. Some people learn better from books, others learn better from doing something hands-on. Some people love going out at night, others are happier staying in. Some people prefer thin-crust pizza, other people (somehow) prefer deep-dish. So why should everyone want the same kind of career?

Be ready to tell the doubters that 9-to-5 jobs work for a lot of people. But that doesn't mean that they need to work for you. Some people like the stability of a 9-to-5; some people find that stifling and crave more flexibility. Some people prefer knowing exactly what their paycheck will be every week; others find it much more motivating to chase commissions, knowing that their rewards will be directly tied to how hard they work. Some people don't like taking on any more risk than they absolutely have to; others are willing to take big risks to achieve bigger dreams. And if I'm not a sleazy, cutthroat person now, what makes you think that I'm going to turn into one the second I get a real estate license?

Unfortunately, some people will never come around, no matter how well you state your case. Some people just want to be right. They want to be able to say, "I told you so." And so, they'll tell you that you're going to fail over and over again, so that if and when you do, they can be there to enjoy the smug satisfaction of having been right all along.

The scary part is, the more you hang around these people who keep telling you you're going to fail, the more likely it becomes that they'll be right.

See, in order to succeed in real estate you need to be motivated, positive, and above all, confident. You need to believe in yourself and what you're selling. Remember that time you bought a house from that guy who was shaking, sweating bullets, stammering, and telling you that he "kinda, sorta" thought it was up to code and "maybe, possibly" thought it was in a safe neighborhood? Neither do I.

But at the same time, it's perfectly normal to be nervous the first few times you take a client out to see a property. People get nervous when they're doing something new, and doubly so if money is on the line. So it's very possible that you might strike out with your first few clients just from nerves.

And even when you get over those early jitters, no one in the history of real estate has ever closed a deal with every single client they've ever worked with. No one. Everyone has bad days. Everyone has slumps. Everyone has those times when they do everything right, but the client just flakes out for some unforeseeable reason. And when that happens, you need to stay positive so you can brush off the disappointment, get back out there, and go find yourself another deal.

It's a lot harder to do that when you hear your friend's voice telling you that you're going to fail echoing around in your head. Instead, every little setback quickly starts to feel like the universe proving your doubters right, instead of what it is: a minor bump on the road to success. It's all too easy to internalize that doubt coming

from someone else and turn it into self-doubt, and agents who are plagued by self-doubt are, more often than not, agents who quit.

That's why, if you have a doubter in your life who just won't change their tune, the healthiest thing you can do is to take some time away from that person. Get that negativity out of your life before it infects you. You can always rekindle the relationship in a little while, once your real estate career is on solid footing and you've got some closed deals under your belt. Because people can argue with just about anything, but they can't argue with results.

Finding Your Style

What works for one salesman may not work for another

Pop quiz: How do you sell a brand-new, spacious, move-in-ready, four-bedroom, four-bath home with high-end appliances and fixtures, gorgeous views, and easy access to shops and restaurants, in a top-ranking school district, that's priced 20 percent below market value?

Answer: You don't. It sells itself.

If every property were like the one I just described, real estate would be the easiest job in the world. Unfortunately, most properties aren't like that. In fact, almost no properties are like that. If you've ever watched an episode of *House Hunters* or a similar show, you know that, even on TV, finding a home almost always means compromising, either on the price, the location, the features of the home, or some combination of the above. Being a real estate salesperson is all about the art of getting people to identify what's really important to them and to accept compromise in order to get the things they want the most.

A little later in this chapter, I'll give you some strategies for combating some of the most common objections that clients raise when they don't want to compromise. But first, let's talk about developing your sales style.

At its core, selling is about influencing people and creating some degree of pressure. People don't like to think of it that way, because that's where we get the image of the pushy, obnoxious, fast-talking salesperson, but that's exactly what it is. If you're not creating any kind of pressure that's directing your client toward making a decision, you're not really selling anything, and you can't be surprised if you don't generate any results.

Every client is different, and you have to constantly adapt your sales techniques to fit them—a client with low credit and income who needs to move tomorrow is going to respond very differently than a client with high credit and income who has a flexible move-in date, for instance—but you also have to find a sales style that works for you.

Sales tactics generally fall into one of two categories: **high pressure** (also called **the hard sell**) and **low pressure** (also called **the soft sell**).

High-pressure sales tactics are ones where the salesperson openly tries to direct the client toward making a purchase, usually by pushing them to make an emotional, impulsive decision rather than one based on factual information. At their worst, high-pressure tactics can amount to little more than the salesperson knocking the client off balance by talking circles around them, keeping them so disoriented that they end up buying something they don't want without asking enough questions or thinking through their decision. This is precisely where the notion of the pushy salesperson comes from.

Imagine a car salesman who tells you that the car you want is normally $20,000, but if you buy it today, they can get you a special, limited-time price of only $18,000. Now the salesperson has just created a time crunch (the limited-time offer) and an incentive (the $2,000 savings). You're nervous about losing out on the special price, and you're excited about the savings, because saving money makes you feel like you're scoring a victory against the car dealership, and that feels really good. So you take the deal, never even realizing that the actual price of the car was $18,000

to begin with, and the salesman had inflated the price to offer you phony savings.

These days, many people go into any interaction with a salesperson expecting the hard sell. People are a lot more knowledgeable about these tactics than they used to be. With the benefit of any number of informational and review services at their fingertips, people today are basically walking bullshit detectors. For instance, in the example above, who goes to buy a car without looking at prices online anymore? If you try to push someone into buying something they don't really want, they're much more likely to stop you in your tracks, walk away, and go work with someone else. Kiss your commission goodbye.

But that doesn't mean that high-pressure sales tactics are dead, or that they can't still be effective, or even that they're always malicious.

In real estate terms, high-pressure sales techniques could be used to rush a client into taking an apartment or a home before they're really ready, or before they've fully explored their options. A common tactic is the old "There are a lot of people interested in this apartment, and I don't want you to miss out on this opportunity" cliché. These tactics can still be very effective, but if you use them, don't expect repeat business or referrals from that client.

That's not to say there's no place for high-pressure sales techniques in real estate, just so long as you're being honest. At their best, the salespeople who utilize high-pressure selling are high energy and infectiously enthusiastic by nature, and they translate that energy into getting their clients enthusiastic, too.

I've known some salespeople who could get you excited about buying shoelaces, because they seem so genuinely excited by the prospect of you owning new shoelaces. In most cases, it's a good thing these people found work in real estate, a field where they get to be on their feet, moving, and meeting new people all the time. These people would take a client out to see an apartment, and then they'd be back in a flash with their clients practically jumping out of their skin to fill out an application.

As long as they were getting these clients excited about apartments that actually worked for them, there was nothing wrong with that. It's only a problem if you're using that kind of enthusiasm and charisma to get people excited about homes they can't afford, ones that aren't safe (either because they are structurally unsound or because you are intentionally misrepresenting the safety of the neighborhood to make a sale), or ones that don't fit their needs. As long as you keep the client's best interests at heart, there's no reason that an emotional appeal can't work for you.

On the other hand, I've also known agents who don't try to appeal to their client's emotions at all. In a few cases, I've had agents who barely even speak to their clients; they give them a little advance information about the apartment they're about to show them, then once they get there, the agents just open the door and stand there in the entryway, letting the client explore on their own and the apartment (and the client's imagination) speak for itself.

Broadly speaking, low-pressure techniques focus more on educating the client, presenting them with the facts, and letting them reach their own conclusion. The above example is low-pressure sales tactics taken to their extreme. (I mean, what's lower pressure than not saying anything at all?) Not everyone can make this tactic work for them, but everyone can educate their clients.

In real estate, educating your client begins with helping them figure out what they really want. Most people have a rough idea of their perfect home in their mind, but they don't really flesh it out until someone pushes them to do it. In your first conversation with the client, you should get them talking about what they want—the things that are absolute must-haves, the things that would be nice bonus features, and the things they don't care about or flat-out don't want. Many times, this list will end up being inaccurate; they might tell you that stainless steel appliances would be a nice perk, but aren't necessary, only to turn around and reject an apartment that has everything else on their wish list because the oven isn't stainless steel. Sometimes people have to face a decision head on to

know what's important to them. But having that initial conversation is a good place to start.

The next part of educating your clients is teaching them about the market. If their budget is $1,500 per month for a two-bedroom apartment, but two-bedroom apartments in the neighborhood they want go for $2,500 and up, you're not doing them any favors by failing to tell them that what they're looking for doesn't exist. It's much more helpful to explain what's happening with the market and educate them about some alternatives. For example: "Neighborhood X may be out of your price range, but Neighborhood Y is along the same train line, has a lot of great bars and restaurants like you wanted, and has a lot more apartments within your budget."

Setting proper expectations for neighborhoods, properties, and even the steps involved in applying for an apartment or putting in an offer on a home will not only put your client in a better position to make an intelligent decision; it will also help you earn the client's trust. When they realize that you want them to be informed, they'll understand that (a) you have their best interest at heart, and (b) you know what you're talking about. They will want to consult you, and they'll value your opinion, which means you can influence their decision-making process without having to resort to emotional manipulation or bluster.

Low-pressure selling is not without its own risks. It's a slower process, for one thing, and creating too little pressure can give a client the leeway to stretch their search on forever, always wanting to wait for more properties to come on the market in case their perfect place should suddenly appear. But when used correctly, low-pressure selling leaves clients feeling empowered, which leads to more repeat business and referrals.

Here's a real example from clients I worked with years ago: The clients, a couple in their early twenties, were moving to Brooklyn from New Jersey. They wanted to be near the Q train for commuting to work. They had been searching for a one-bedroom apartment on their own for a while, but weren't finding anything,

in part because they didn't know enough about the less-famous neighborhoods of Brooklyn to know where to look.

I took them to see an apartment in an up-and-coming neighborhood along the Q train that was renting for $950 a month (it's a sign of just how long ago this was that it was possible to get a one-bedroom anywhere in Brooklyn for that little). They loved the feel of the area, and they immediately connected with the apartment, which had a funky layout that gave it a lot of character. It had odd angles and a lot of overhead storage instead of traditional closets, all of which gave it an unusual, old-world feel that the couple clearly enjoyed.

If I were using high-pressure tactics, I could have ended their search right then and there. I could have capitalized on their obvious affection for the apartment to get them to put down a deposit and fill out an application at that moment, there's not a shred of doubt in my mind about that. But while I think they certainly could have made that apartment work for them, I had a couple of concerns.

For one, they were moving from a house in New Jersey to an apartment in Brooklyn. If they were moving with a lot of furniture, would it fit the odd angles in this apartment? And second, both of the people in this couple were pretty short, and those overhead storage spaces were pretty high up. They said they could deal with the overhead storage, but that felt like it might be their enthusiasm talking. Would they really want to have to pull out a stepladder anytime they needed to get something out of their closets? My fear was that they would get sick of it after a week and end up with buyer's (or rather, renter's) remorse, which would be unfortunate for them and almost certainly mean no future business for me.

Instead, I took them to see another apartment a couple stops further along the Q line. The neighborhood didn't have quite as much going for it, but it was safe, quiet, and had everything they needed, like grocery stores, pharmacies, and a handful of places to eat out. The apartment was a little cheaper, at $900 a month, but it was a little further from the train and there was nothing interesting about it at all. It was the most straightforward, simple architecture you can imagine, a railroad-style one-bedroom that was basically one cube-shaped room that led straight into another. The drab paint on the walls felt like it came from the hallway of a mental hospital. It was a good amount of usable space, but I could tell it didn't excite them. I could see they were still thinking about the first apartment.

I took the time to sit down with them and make a list of pros and cons for the two apartments, encouraging them to think about the practicalities of living in each one. Although they both started out excited about the first apartment with all the character, by the time they'd finished listing the pros and cons, they were surprised to find out that the second apartment came out ahead.

They ended up taking the second apartment. Because it was less expensive, it meant I received a smaller commission than I would have with the first apartment. But the couple was very happy there (they ended up living there for three years), and the next time they had a friend moving to New York, they put him in touch with me. I was able to find their friend an apartment as well. So, because I went with a low-pressure technique—guiding them toward the facts instead of capitalizing on their emotions—I ended up making an additional commission, coming out ahead in the long run.

In truth, you'll most likely end up utilizing a combination of high- and low-pressure sales techniques to fit your clients and, more importantly, to fit your personality. If you're a low-key person by nature, trying to get your clients super psyched up about an apartment could easily come across as too forced. At the other end of the spectrum, if you're the sort of person who can't sit still, you probably don't have the calm, collected demeanor to pull off something like standing silently in the doorway and letting the clients explore the apartment on their own; they'd just end up getting freaked out by you standing there, fidgeting.

Take a moment to think back to times when you've convinced someone to do something or change their mind about something.

It doesn't have to have been convincing them to buy something, it could be as simple as getting them to agree with your point of view in an argument.

How did you do it? Did you work an emotional angle to make them think with their heart instead of their head? Did you hammer them with facts until they threw up their hands and gave up? Did you poke holes in their argument until they decided they ought to switch their position? Did you present your case and let them come to their own conclusion (which, of course, was the conclusion you wanted them to reach)?

However you did it, that might be the foundation of your personal sales style. It will take you some time—and probably some trial and error—to craft your sales style, and to get comfortable enough with your own strengths that you can adapt on the fly to fit your clients' individuals needs and circumstances. But once you find your style, everything else is just details.

The Salesman's Schedule

Why time management is the key to real estate success

As a real estate broker, there are a thousand different things to keep track of at any given moment. There are calls and emails to and from buyers, sellers, renters, and landlords; ads to post, showings, closings, lease signings, open houses, and the daily search for new listings. Managing your time well is the biggest key to success in this business. It's especially important when you're first starting out, so that you develop good work habits early on.

A lot of people get into real estate sales thinking it's something they can do part-time, either while working another job or doing something else on the side. To be sure, I've known some wildly successful agents who only worked part-time. They were the sort of agents who could go out on one showing and come back with a deposit with staggering consistency. But that kind of skill level is incredibly rare. And each and every one of those agents who was able to be successful doing real estate part-time started out by doing it around the clock.

So, maybe you'll end up becoming one of those exception-to-the-rule agents who knocks it out of the park with every client so often that you can make the kind of money you want to make in real estate while only working part-time. I know a lot of agents who will be jealous of you. But don't expect to reach that level right away.

Starting a real estate career means you're taking a chance on yourself. So give yourself the best chance you can and commit to it full-time, especially at the beginning.

Here's a simple schedule you can follow to make the most of your day. This is geared toward agents working in rentals, but it can easily be adapted for sales:

7:00–9:00 AM: Post ads. Many of the most popular sites organize their ads in the order in which they were submitted, meaning the sooner someone searches that sight after you post your ad, the higher up in the search rankings your ad will be. A lot of people who are searching for a new home do their online searches while they're eating breakfast, or right when they arrive to work, so this is a good time to get your ads out there to catch those morning searchers.

9:00–10:00 AM: Training. Take some time to wake up your brain and get excited for your day by learning something new about your business. If your company offers daily training, great. If not, there are tons of places online to pick up new sales techniques or learn about the latest market trends. Whether you're reading an article, watching a video, listening to a podcast, or engaging in an in-person training session, use this time to sharpen your skills.

10:00 AM–12:00 PM: Plan out your day. Clear out your voicemails and your email inbox. Get back to any clients who asked you to contact them. If you have showings scheduled for later in the day, contact the landlords, supers, or whoever else you need to speak to in order to make sure you have access. If you don't have four to five appointments set up with clients for that day, contact any clients you can to fill out your appointment schedule. Confirm the appointments you already have on the books.

12:00–2:00 PM: Post ads. If you haven't set up your appointments by this time in the day, it can be a lot harder to do it now. By lunchtime, people generally have their whole day planned out in their heads, and it can be tough to get them to change it. Even if their plans for the evening are "sit on couch, do nothing," by this point in the day, they're looking forward to that. However, this is a great time to post some more ads, because people also tend to search real estate listings on their lunch breaks.

2:00–5:00 PM: Preparation and early appointments. This is the key time for taking out clients who took a half day from work or school to go see some listings. Often this means the client is in a serious rush to find a new place to live. It could also be that the apartment you want to show them is only available to be seen at this time. This is particularly common in areas with large Jewish populations, where a landlord may not be able to schedule any showings after sundown on a Friday for religious reasons.

If you don't have any appointments in this time slot, use this time to get organized for your appointments coming up in the evening. Where are you meeting them? What route will you take? What features of the neighborhood will you show them? If there are any details about how to access the apartments that you still need to clear up, such as a keycode or confirming a meeting time with a landlord, now's the time to do it.

And if you don't have any appointments lined up at all, use this time to try to book some last-minute showings. If that doesn't work, it's never a bad idea to post some more ads, to get a head start on preparing for tomorrow's appointments, or to go out and familiarize yourself with your company's inventory by visiting properties. And it's never a bad time to go out looking for new listings!

5:00–7:00 PM: Appointment time! Ideally, you should have four to five appointments booked for the evening. This is the most popular timeslot for showings. People get out of work and they want to do their apartment hunting before heading home for the night. Landlords love it when you bring them clients who are coming straight from work. Why? Because it means they have a job! Rush hour means traffic could be a nightmare, so be sure to factor that into your travel time. For each appointment, plan on showing them one apartment, plus one to two backups in case they don't love the first one as much as they thought from your ad.

7:00–9:00 PM: Late appointments. The later it gets in the evening, the more difficult it can be to get access to apartments that require a landlord or super to let you in, because they're ready to call it a day. On the other hand, it's often the best time to get access to apartments that are still occupied, where the outgoing tenant has agreed to let you in, because they are now home from work.

If you're not out on appointments, it's a great time to post ads to catch people who are getting serious about their search. At this time of day, people who are looking at real estate listings aren't doing it casually to amuse themselves while they're scarfing down a meal; they're making a point to take time out of the evening to see what's on the market.

9:00–10:00 PM: Look ahead. This is the time to set yourself up for success tomorrow. Send yourself anything you need to be able to access from home, if you can't get it wirelessly. Organize your leads and appointments for tomorrow. But most importantly, take a little time to reflect on your day. How did you do? Did you get as many appointments as you wanted to? Did they go the way you hoped? What did you do well? What could you improve on? There will always be circumstances that are out of your control, like a

client canceling on you at the last minute, so don't waste time worrying about things like that. Focus on yourself, and what you want to do better tomorrow.

Why five appointments? Five appointments may sound like a lot, especially if you could end up showing each client as many as three apartments apiece. I recommend aiming for five appointments a day for a few reasons:

1. Because it's much better to have too many appointments than too few. Worst-case scenario, if you have more appointments than you can reasonably handle, you can probably get another agent in your office to take one off your hands and agree to split the commission.

2. Because someone almost always cancels or stands you up. I can't tell you how many times I've seen agents just sitting around the office because they had only one appointment booked, and then the client bailed on them due to some unforeseen circumstance (and just to be clear, "unforeseen circumstance" doesn't always mean an emergency; clients will often cancel just because they suddenly decide they don't feel like seeing apartments that day).

3. So that even if you fall short, you still have three to four appointments lined up.

Types of Clients

Meet some of the people you'll be seeing
every single day in real estate

Every client is unique...up to a point. You won't have to be in this business for long before you start to recognize certain archetypes that repeat over and over. Understanding what type of client you're dealing with can help you quickly and easily determine the best way to help them. Here are some of the most common clients you'll encounter.

Ready to Make a Decision

Let's get this one out of the way first, because it's the easiest, although unfortunately not the most common. Sometimes you get a client who's been looking for a long time, and is ready to just be done with it. They have all their paperwork together, they have all their finances together; if you can find them something they can live with, they'll take it. Let them know that you understand how they feel, that you get that looking for a home is like having a second job, and now you're going to take that burden off their shoulders.

When you get a client who's truly ready to make a decision from the first contact you have with them, drop what you're doing and help them. If every client were like this, real estate would be the easiest job in the world.

The Out-of-Towner

They're moving from another city, they'll only be in town for a couple of days, and the only thing they're here to do is look for a place to live. When an out-of-town client gives you a call, it's like a gift falling into your lap. You couldn't ask for a more motivated client. All they want to do is find someplace before they have to go back home. That's a highly stressful scenario to be in, especially if they don't know their new, soon-to-be home city very well yet, so they will be extremely grateful for your help.

It's important to lock in an appointment (or even multiple appointments) early with an out-of-town client, because it's very likely that they'll be contacting multiple agents from multiple companies.

The most important thing you can do for an out-of-town client is to set realistic expectations well in advance. Someone moving from a small town to a big city, for instance, can easily get massive sticker shock if you don't give them a real sense of what they can get for their money ahead of time.

But if you take the time to educate your clients, show them around, really make them feel like they're making an informed decision, they'll genuinely appreciate it, and that appreciation can very easily translate into referrals or repeat business.

The Dreamer

A dreamer is a client who wants something they can't have. Sometimes it's simply that they don't know any better—for instance, someone who's moving out of their parents' place and has never had to know anything about the market before. But just as often, it's someone who saw people living in a giant, impossibly cheap apartment on TV and believes there must be something like that out there for them.

Watch out for phrases like "My friend has a place just up the block for [insert unrealistically low amount]," or "I saw an ad for an apartment for [insert unrealistically low amount] in this neighborhood online the other day." If their friend really lives in a building that's priced so far below market value, why aren't they asking their friend if their landlord has any vacancies? If they really saw an apartment being advertised for so little, why didn't they respond to that ad, instead of responding to yours?

The fact is, sometimes people hear something thirdhand, or they catch a piece of a conversation out of context, or they misunderstand something they read somewhere, or sometimes they literally dream something up out of thin air, and they convince themselves it's true. You're not doing them or yourself any favors by playing along. You're a real estate professional. You're the one with expert knowledge of the market. It's much kinder in the long run to tell them straight, "For the neighborhood you want, apartments go for X to Y dollars," to get them to understand the reality of their situation so you can show them something in a different

neighborhood that they could actually afford, than to spend weeks showing them places they would never qualify for.

Just Started

When a client has just started looking for a place to live, they may feel like they have all the time in the world. But in a competitive market—and where isn't a competitive market these days?—if they don't get serious in a hurry, they could find themselves in a tight spot. It's your job to educate them and earn their trust (two things that go hand-in-hand), and get them to appreciate the constraints of the market in order to generate a realistic sense of urgency.

Just understand that they might not respond to, or appreciate, any attempt to rush them into a decision. Even if they love an apartment, someone who just started looking might not be heartbroken about letting it pass them by, because they think there's another one around the corner. But if they let one place pass them by, and the next place doesn't measure up, that can easily ramp up their stress level.

The Shopper

The shopper doesn't need to move right away. They're just looking to see what's out there. It's usually someone with at least four months left before their target move date, and often with enough of a budget that they can afford to be picky. They might not be motivated to go after a property unless it meets literally every single criterion they have, from the most important must-have features to the tiniest wouldn't-it-be-nice.

This could end up being a long-term relationship, so don't rush it. A shopper won't respond favorably to pressure. They'll interpret it as you getting desperate for a commission, and they'll take their business elsewhere. So let them take it slow. You can even offer to help them shop around. Just don't let a shopper chew up too much of your time. While their higher budget may ultimately mean a higher commission, it's still just one deal, so you can't let yourself get swept up in the notion of a big payday. If it starts to feel like the shopper is acting like you work directly for them, and like they're the only client who could possibly matter, even though they're not actually compensating you for your time, it's time to pull back and focus on other clients for a while.

Oh, and never call them a shopper to their face. Let's keep that just between us, okay?

Roommates

Roommate situations can be tricky. They come in all shapes and sizes, from couples moving in together for the first time to students who all have guarantors covering their rent, to friends moving to a new city together, to complete strangers who found one another on Craigslist.

The one thing that all roommate situations have in common is this: no matter how much they say they're all equals in the decision-making process, someone is always in charge. It's rarely an official position, and it may not be just one person, but there is always at least one decision maker.

Your job will be a lot easier, and everyone will end up much happier, if you can determine who the decision maker is. It's not always the person who makes the most money. I've seen plenty of couples where only one person was employed and would be paying for the apartment single-handedly, but the other person in the couple was actually the one who called the shots. It's not even necessarily the person who speaks up the most, or who does the most work as far as organizing trips to go look at properties. The decision maker can often be the quiet one who says he or she doesn't care, and will do whatever everyone else in the group wants, but then says no to everything when the time comes to make a final call about a place.

With couples, identifying the decision maker is generally pretty simple. It's larger roommate scenarios that can be tricky, especially if not every roommate shows up for every showing appointment. Try as hard as you can to get everyone to commit to showing up in advance, and if there's anyone who can't make it, try to get them to agree to let the group make a decision without them, as long as there is a consensus.

There's also the fact that very, very few apartments with multiple bedrooms have bedrooms that are all the same size. Some are wildly different. Will the roommates all be paying an equal share, no matter what? Or will they pay proportional amounts, and divide up the rooms accordingly? Making sure all the roommates are on the same page about these things can save a lot of time and arguing.

Overcoming Objections

How to get your clients to see an imperfect
property in a new light

Here's the one and only thing you need to know about the perfect home: it doesn't exist. A place could always use a few more square feet, a few more windows, an extra closet. It could always be a little closer to the train or a little farther from noise. This is especially true in a densely populated city like New York, where people are crammed on top of one another and the competition for real estate—any real estate—can be ferocious.

Learning to overcome your clients' objections is not about getting them to take a place that doesn't work for them. If a place isn't the right fit for someone, it's not the right fit, and trying to push them into taking a place where they wouldn't be happy is as shady as it gets.

But every objection is also an opportunity. It's an opportunity to help your clients see things from a different perspective when reality doesn't match up to the picture they had in their head. It's an opportunity to help them to overlook a surface problem to see the potential in a home that could actually be great for them. It's

about doing your part to ensure that they don't miss out on a great place because they got hung up on its imperfections.

You know the saying, "Give me the serenity to accept the things I cannot change, the courage to change the things I can, and the wisdom to know the difference?" Well, sometimes that wisdom needs to come from an agent.

Pro tip: Never preemptively assume your client has a particular objection. Everyone has different priorities and different opinions. You might walk into an apartment and immediately think, "There's no closet, it's too small, and climbing all the stairs to get up here nearly killed me." But your client could have a clothing rack all ready to go and could be an exercise enthusiast who loves being outside and runs stairs for fun. I'll always tell you to put yourself in your client's shoes, but when it comes to objections, respond to the objections your client actually has, not the ones you think they ought to have.

Here are some of the most common objections, and tips for how to handle them:

It's Too Small!

Working in New York City, this is probably the most common objection you hear. A lot of apartments are small, and sometimes it seems like they're constantly building them smaller.

Obviously, the size of an apartment is one of those things that can't be changed. But it can be put in perspective. First of all, there are more creative, space-saving storage solutions available today than ever before, and most of them are very affordable. End tables, coffee tables, and even chairs, beds, and couches are all available with built-in storage these days. Creative shelving can also dramatically add to the amount of usable space.

Oftentimes the complaint won't be about the whole apartment, but the size of one of the bedrooms. The client will say, "I can't get my [X]-sized bed in here." That's when it's useful to

have a tape measure on hand, and to familiarize yourself with the measurements of different beds.

- **Twin**—39×75 inches (or 99×190 cm)
- **X-Long Twin**—39×80 inches (or 99×203 cm)
- **Full**—54×75 inches (or 137×190 cm)
- **Queen**—60×80 inches (or 153×203 cm)
- **King**—76×80 inches (or 198×203 cm)

Go ahead and measure the room right then and there. Have your client help you. If the room really isn't big enough…well… unless the client is willing to downsize their bed, the complaint is legitimate, and there's not a lot you can do except to move on. But a lot of times, a room looks smaller than it is for whatever reason. Sometimes rooms just look small. Clients will often be surprised to find just how easily their bed really could fit in there, and how much space would still be left over.

And possibly the best way to overcome this objection is to remind the client why they want to live there in the first place. This is especially true for out-of-town clients who are moving to the city for the first time. Someone moving from the Midwest to New York might be completely shocked, because $2,000 a month would get them a huge house where they live now, but might get them only five hundred square feet in a prime neighborhood of Brooklyn.

Remind them that they're not moving to the city for its spacious apartments. They're moving there to take advantage of everything there is to do outside those four walls. Take them around the neighborhood and show them some of the wonderful things that would be just outside their door. Sell them on the location and its amenities, and they'll quickly realize that there's so much to do, all they really need from an apartment is a place to sleep.

There Are No/Not Enough Closets!

This one goes right along with "too small," in the sense that you can't change it, but you can make it a little easier to swallow.

Again, this is where understanding storage solutions really comes in handy. You can't magically create a closet for them, but you can show them a smart place to put a dresser, or help them visualize a system of racks and hooks that they could easily install.

I've known some agents who carry an IKEA catalogue around with them at all times, just so they can whip it out to show clients the latest build-it-yourself storage ideas. In fact, IKEA is just one of many furniture companies these days that specialize in urban living, meaning they know how to squeeze the most out of small spaces. Take the time to familiarize yourself, so you can familiarize your clients if you need to.

The Building is Too Old!

Many clients picture themselves living in sleek, ultramodern high rises, and they don't want to look at anything else. But it's the older, prewar buildings that give a lot of cities their charm. If your client scoffs at living in a prewar building, here are a few things to point out:

For starters, prewar buildings are usually really well-constructed. That's how they've stayed up for so long. The walls are typically thick and solid, which means you don't overhear every conversation your neighbor is having, or accidentally hear *Game of Thrones* spoilers because they left their TV on. When you've had a long day and just need to unwind in peace and quiet, that's a major plus.

Older buildings usually include heat and hot water in the rent, because there is a central boiler that can't be controlled by the tenant. That means significant savings on your client's utility bills—possibly hundreds of dollars every month.

Because of trends in construction and the simple fact that landlords know they can charge more for newer units, apartments in older buildings are often larger than newer apartments that cost the same amount of money, so you get more space for your buck.

Older buildings contain a lot of wonderful design elements

that you just don't see in newer structures. Point out architectural elements like tin ceilings, crown mouldings, art deco details in the lobby, or anything else that shows off the building's vintage touches. When clients feel like the building is a part of the history and fabric of a city, they will often view it in a new light.

The Building is Too New!

Just as there are clients who want to live somewhere modern, there are clients who picture themselves living in a vintage brownstone. They think newer buildings are soulless boxes that lack character, and they don't like that newer buildings tend to make tenants pay for their own utilities. When you have a client who wants old-world charm, but all you have to show them is modern convenience, here are a few things to mention.

Yes, newer buildings tend to make the tenants pay for their own utilities, but that's because they actually get to control their own utilities. No more waiting for the landlord to decide whether it's cold enough that the heat deserves to be turned on, or warm enough that it's time to turn it back off (which is much worse, in my opinion). The client would have their own thermostat, so they could decide exactly what they want the temperature to be. And most thermostats these days have built-in timers, making it easy to keep costs down by turning off the heat during the hours of the day when no one is at home.

Apartments in prewar buildings may tend to be a little cheaper than newer constructions, but apartments in the kind of classic brownstones that most Old World lovers picture themselves in are actually hugely expensive, due to the rarity and demand.

New buildings are, well, new, and that comes with some perks. For instance, you don't have to worry about appliances breaking down, because they don't have any wear and tear yet. You also don't have to worry about dealing with damage accumulated over years of use by other tenants, such as damaged walls or floors, or

sometimes even rats or roaches that have been attracted by years of reliable food.

A brand-new apartment may not have the character that your client was hoping for, but that doesn't mean they can't give it character of their own. A brand-new apartment is a blank slate, just waiting for someone to come along and make their mark.

And of course, be sure to capitalize on any modern amenities that the client might not be able to find in an older building, such as fitness centers, laundry, dishwashers, video intercoms, security systems, recessed lighting, green features like bamboo floors or energy-efficient appliances—heck, some new buildings even include wi-fi in the rent.

It's Too High Up!

You'll generally get this complaint from people looking at apartments on the upper floors of walk-up buildings. They take a look at all those stairs, picture themselves moving in with all their stuff, or having to deal with the stairs at the end of a long day, and they just throw up their hands and say forget about it.

The truth is, though, living on a high floor comes with its share of real advantages:

- Top-floor apartments don't have to deal with people walking above them.
- If the building has an accessible roof, you're that much closer. Everyone loves being able to hang out on the roof, looking out at the skyline.
- Higher floors usually have more natural light.
- Higher floors often have better breezes in the summer (if you're showing an apartment with a good cross-breeze in the dead of summer, that can be enough to close the deal right then and there).
- Everyone likes a room with a view.
- Since heat rises, the upper floors usually require less

heating, which means savings if the tenant controls their own heat.

- Better privacy.
- Less noise, since you're further from the street.
- Upper-floor apartments are generally safer than ones on the lower levels.
- Upper-floor apartments are also less susceptible to pests and vermin than lower floors.
- Finally, all those stairs stop being a nuisance after a while. You get used to them remarkably quickly. And the health benefits from going up and down those stairs mean you don't even need a gym membership!

It's on the Ground Floor!

People have concerns about ground-floor apartments. They picture them as dark and noisy (both from the street and from people coming and going all day and night), and they worry about the security risks if the unit has doors or windows that open right onto the street.

But there are plenty of perks to living in a ground-floor apartment, too:

- Moving in and out is much easier.
- It's a lot easier and less exhausting when you're coming in with groceries, laundry, or packages.
- You get to avoid that dreaded moment at the end of a long day when you finally get in the front door, only to have to climb five flights of stairs.
- Being on a lower floor means quick access into and out of the building if there's ever an emergency, and will definitely make your life easier if you should ever hurt yourself and have trouble walking.
- Got kids? Got a stroller? Want to lug it up five flights

while holding your passed-out toddler in the other hand? Didn't think so.

• Ground-floor apartments may have access to a yard, garden, or other outdoor space.

A lot of these advantages are erased if the building has an elevator, I grant you. But if you've ever seen the looks on people's faces in a high-rise building when the elevator breaks down, you know that elevators aren't everything.

One Roommate Hates It!

Sometimes it seems like no matter how many apartments you show a group of roommates, there's one guy who always finds something to hate, and as soon as he does, even if it's minor, everyone else just gives in. I talked earlier about finding the decision maker in the group. Well, you found him.

If everyone else in the group likes the place, but one guy makes a single negative comment about the paint color and everyone else seems like they're not willing to fight, it's usually because the group knows their own dynamic well enough to know that once this guy starts nitpicking, there's nowhere to go but down.

You should always exercise caution when inserting yourself into a group dynamic—it's surprisingly easy to find the whole group turned against you, the outsider—but if one person is consistently problematic, sometimes the best thing to do is to remind the others that it may be easier to find another roommate than to find another apartment that they all like.

The goal here is not to split up the group. You don't want to be the jerk who butted in and ruined a friendship. And besides, if you're dealing with four people, and one of them gets kicked out, now you'll have to start all over again, helping them find three-bedroom apartments instead of four-bedroom ones.

Instead, what you're trying to do is remind them that they've already gotten past the toughest part of the apartment hunt—finding a good place. Do they really want to let it pass them by? In many cases, just bringing this to their attention will be enough to get them to at least consider the possibility of finding a new roommate to replace the one who's refusing to cooperate. And that will often get the troublesome roommate to change his tune and go with the rest of the group, which was the goal all along.

I Like It, But...

There's no way to prepare for every possible objection a client could raise. I've been in this business for nearly two decades, and I'm still surprised with the reasons people come up with to turn down a perfectly good place.

The fact of the matter is, sometimes clients will turn down an apartment just to prolong their search. It seems crazy—when have you ever met someone in the middle of house hunting who says they wish it would take longer?—but it's true. Even after looking at countless places, they're afraid that if they take a place that meets 95 percent of their criteria today, a place that meets 100 percent of their criteria will come on the market tomorrow. And it will be cheaper. And closer to the subway.

That's why learning to overcome objections is so important. I've known plenty of agents who don't even try to rebut their clients' objections. As soon as they client says something negative, they just whisk them out the door to the next place. Those agents are also typically the most exhausted and have the worst showing-to-closing ratios. You can end up putting a huge amount of time into a single client and seeing more apartments than you ever thought possible while basically watching your client hunt for that elusive "perfect" apartment, or you can do the job you signed up to do and actually help them find something real.

The single most common reaction to an apartment from a client who's not quite ready to make a decision is, "I like it, but..."

That phrase is an opportunity in disguise. "I like it, but I wish it had a bigger kitchen." "I like it, but I wish the bathroom were updated." "I like it, but I wish it were closer to the train." When you hear this phrase, your response should be, "So, if I found you an apartment just like this one, but the kitchen was bigger/bathroom were updated/it were closer to the train, you'd take it?"

That puts the client in the mindset to make a decision, which is the most important step in the process. If you have another apartment lined up that fits the description (or you know how to get access to one in a hurry), that's your next stop. If not, your appointment is done for the day. Head back to the office and start looking through your inventory so you can show them exactly what they're looking for tomorrow. And if there's nothing that fits the bill in your inventory already, hit the streets and go find it.

The Elevator Pitch

There is no more critical tool in the broker's arsenal than a good elevator pitch. If you're not familiar, an elevator pitch is a twenty-to-thirty-second statement explaining who you are, what you do, and why it's unique. The idea is simple enough: you step into an elevator with a potential client. How do you convince them to work with you by the time the doors open again?

Of course, an elevator pitch is not just for elevators. It could be something you bust out while walking to your car, or while standing in line for a taxi, or while waiting for a table at a restaurant, or while getting ready to board a plane. It's something you could end up cycling through fifty different times at a networking event. Anytime you have someone's attention for a short period of time, you can capitalize on that opportunity if you have your elevator pitch down pat.

Crafting the perfect elevator pitch is a tricky thing. Entire books have been written on the subject, and there are experts out there (as well as plenty of people passing themselves off as experts) who give lectures on this topic every single day. There's no 100-percent-perfect recipe, but there are common building blocks you can use to gather your thoughts and put them into action.

The first step is simply determining who this elevator pitch is for. Who's your intended audience, and what are you trying to get them to do? As a real estate broker, you'll need at least two versions of your elevator pitch: one to convince buyers and tenants to work with you, and one to convince landlords and sellers to give you their listings.

Once you've got your audience and your goal settled, it's time to figure out what you're going to tell them. You need to explain who you are and what you do as quickly as possible, but you also need to do it in a way that will grab their attention. As I tell Rapid Realty agents, just saying, "I'm a real estate agent" is boring. Even saying, "I'm an agent with Rapid Realty" is boring—and I'm the guy who started Rapid Realty. But if you say, "I'm an agent with Rapid Realty, the largest apartment rental company in New York"—now you've given your listener something they can sink their teeth into.

Now that you've got your listener interested, it's time to hit them with something special—something only you or your company can offer. Imagine you're a landlord with a vacancy coming up, and you just happen to bump into a real estate agent who says they specialize in rentals. Sounds good, right? But what piece of information would clinch the deal? That's what you want to communicate next, something that you can deliver that all the other real estate companies out there can't. Is it your years of experience? Your technology? Do you have an impressive closing ratio, or an award for the most closed deals in a single month? In other words, if I'm the landlord with a vacancy and I'm listening to you, why should I want to give you my listing right here, right now, instead of going, "Oh yeah, a real estate agent. I should probably talk to one of those."

If you're having trouble coming up with something unique, try this exercise: start with the phrase, "We do things differently. We [_____]." Whatever you used to fill in the blank, that's your unique reason you can give people to prove why they should work with you. It doesn't necessarily have to be that you're

the best in the world, you're just trying to communicate what makes you and your company special at that particular moment.

So, you've hooked your listener with what you do, you've reeled them in with what makes your services unique, now it's time to put the ball back in their court in a way that will leave them engaged. A great way to do this is by ending on a question that could spark further conversation. And the trick to that is simple: get your listener talking about themselves. People love to talk about themselves.

So, instead of giving them a simple yes-or-no question, where they can give you a one-syllable answer and then brush you off, ask them something that will prompt them to start telling you their story. For example, if you're talking to a potential buyer or renter, don't end your elevator pitch with, "Are you working with a broker right now?" That's like asking someone if they have a boyfriend. First of all, it seems desperate, and second of all, they can just say yes and walk away. Instead, try that old favorite, "How long have you been looking?" Anyone who's been searching for a home more than fifteen minutes will be all too happy to share how long and frustrating it's been.

With a landlord or property manager, you would vary it slightly. Try, "How long has it been on the market?" Or, "How long does it usually take you to get your vacancies rented?" With someone selling their house, a classic conversation starter is, "What made you decide to sell?" or its variant, "What made you decide to sell now?" Whether it's financial hardship causing them to downsize or financial gain allowing them to upgrade; a change in their family dynamic; or they're moving for work, school, or just a change of scenery, everyone wants to tell their story, if you give them an opening.

With any luck, you'll strike up a conversation and time and circumstances will allow you to talk long enough for you to secure their business. But whether this is the moment they agree to work with you, or just the beginning of a discussion to be picked up

later, you'll want to leave them with something to remember you by. The best example, of course, is your business card.

You should always keep a supply of current business cards on you whenever you leave the house. No excuses. If I bump into you on the street and you can't give me your card, I'm going to be very disappointed.

But since everyone else in the world has a business card, it also helps to invest in some other small memento you can give out, like a pen with your contact information on it. I've seen people give out everything from keychains and refrigerator magnets to personalized toothpicks (which was, frankly, a little odd—if you don't use it, it's just a pointy stick in your pocket, and if you do use it, who wants to carry a used toothpick around all day?) and beyond. Giving your potential client something that goes that one little step beyond the norm can make a big impression.

Okay, so let's go over the checklist one more time. You're going to identify your target audience and what you hope to gain from them. You're going to introduce yourself and your business. You're going to explain one thing that makes your services unique. You're going to engage them in conversation by getting them talking about themselves. And finally, you're going to give them your card, and possibly something else to remember you by. And you're going to do it all in absolutely no more than thirty seconds.

As you can probably imagine, good elevator pitches don't come together instantly. It takes practice. Once you've crafted your elevator pitch, run through it in a mirror. Run through it with your friends and family. Try it out as many times as you can. Cut out anything that doesn't get right to the point. You want to make it as memorable as possible, not just so your listener will remember talking to you, but also so you won't have to struggle to recall your elevator pitch when you need it. It's not just about going to networking events, after all. An opportunity could literally present itself the next time you step into an elevator.

Will you be ready?

Shaking off a Slump

How to get your real estate mojo back

Everyone—politicians, programmers, professional athletes—hits a slump every now and again. Everyone has the occasional period where it seems like nothing is going right, and nothing they do can create any positive results. But in a commission-based business like real estate, where your pay is directly tied to producing closed deals, hitting a slump can feel like a career-ending disaster. I've been there. And that's exactly why I'm going to tell you how to snap out of it—and how to avoid making it worse.

DO tell yourself that other people have felt the way you're feeling now. When I say that everyone hits slumps, I mean everyone. That means that, sure, everyone who has given up on themselves and quit has felt the way you're feeling, but so have all the greats who pushed past it and went on to achieve their goals. Which one would you rather be?

DON'T wallow in self-pity. When things go wrong, it's very tempting to focus on how the universe is screwing you over, or to play the What If? game, where you sit around thinking about what would have happened in that last deal if one thing or another had gone just a little differently. Pop quiz: how many deals do you think get closed by playing that game? The answer is zero. What happened is what happened. Learn whatever lessons you can from it, even if that lesson is just that sometimes deals die for no good reason (although there's usually a reason, so do try to dig a little deeper than that), and move on.

DO set small, achievable goals. You know why soldiers are required to make their bed a certain, precise way every morning? I mean, it's not like having a well-made bed makes you any better at driving a Humvee, or disarming an IED, or aiming a rifle, right? Well, it's not just to promote unit discipline (although it's certainly a part of

it). It's also because days in the military can be incredibly long and draining, and this ensures that they start things off on a productive note. It's a way to check something off their to-do list right at the start of the day, because we all know that checking things off your to-do list feels great, and motivates you to keep going. So give yourself a list of small, easily managed tasks, so that you can feel that sense of accomplishment as you check things off and get into a positive and productive mindset.

DON'T worry about what other people are doing. There's nothing worse when you're in a slump than watching some other agent in your office landing deal after deal. Don't stress yourself out worrying why you're not having the kind of luck that someone else is having, and why things aren't going that way for you. Motivation comes from within. Focus on your own tasks, and you'll get back in the game faster.

DO cut yourself some slack. You're going to hear "no" a lot in this business. That doesn't mean that every no is a failure. A lot of the time, it's just the price you have to pay before you can get to yes. So don't beat yourself up if your first attempts to shake off your slump don't pan out. Just keep going. And treat yourself every now and again. You're working hard—give yourself the credit you deserve.

DON'T try to be a sharpshooter. There's a common mistake that a lot of agents make when they're trying to get out of a slump: they cherry-pick their clients and the properties they advertise to try to set up a "perfect deal," a home run that will get them back on top in one fell swoop. They delude themselves into thinking that if they can just land that one big fish, everyone will respect them and everything will be great. That may be how it works in movies, but in real life, one deal is still just one deal. If things aren't going your way, it's much better to get back to basics, get yourself back on a regimented schedule, and work on getting those five appointments every day. Give yourself more chances, not fewer.

DO get back on that horse. Slumps last as long as they last. Sometimes you just have to push yourself through a certain number of failed deals and unsuccessful client interactions before you get your game back. Some slumps last longer than others, but there's only one way for them to last forever, and that's if you give up. Believe in yourself enough to trust that you'll find your stride again, then get back out there and prove it.

PART 4

Real Estate Investment 101

Real estate has only fairly recently become a popular investment vehicle for "regular folks." Until the 1950s or so, very few people thought about buying buildings other than their own homes, and owning your home has always been one of the components of the American Dream. Owning rental properties—apartment buildings, office buildings, shopping centers—was once considered the province of institutional investors, like insurance companies or pension funds. In New York City, much of the most desirable real estate belongs to a few very wealthy families.

It's not easy to get into real estate investment if you don't have a lot of capital. But if you're an entrepreneur at heart, if you're a player, if you love to take chances and be the master of your own fate, real estate is the way to go.

Investing in real estate is a lot different from investing in stocks and bonds. Here are some of the differences to consider:

The Minuses

Real estate is not liquid. If you own a stock, you can usually sell it in seconds, with a mouse click or two. This is why day trading is a popular occupation for people who like to live dangerously and who have fast reflexes. Day traders can buy and sell all day, realizing a slight gain on each transaction, and when they close out their positions at the end of that day, if they've played well, they'll

have a nice profit. Even if you're not a day trader, even if you buy stocks to hold them and collect dividends, you'll be able to sell them quickly if a better investment comes along, or if you need capital for some other purpose.

Real estate isn't like that. When you buy a building, you'd better have an idea of how long you'll want to hold onto it, and have an exit strategy in place, because it's not an asset you can count on selling quickly. Even if you need to sell a building in a hurry, it could stay on the market for months, or even years, unless you agree to sell it for less than it's worth.

And meanwhile, your capital will be tied up in it. If you need capital for some emergency, you can sometimes refinance your mortgage, or take out a loan against whatever equity you have in the building—but those deals can be hard to get, and they're seldom cheap.

Real estate involves debt. When you buy a stock, you usually buy it with cash. Some investors buy "on margin," paying only a percentage of a stock's price and owing the rest, but there are strict rules about the extent to which you can employ that strategy, and for most investors a stock purchase is an all-cash deal. A real estate transaction is seldom all cash. If you're buying your own home, you'll typically pay 25 percent of the price in cash—also known as equity, in this context—and pay off the rest on a thirty-year mortgage. Prior to the mortgage meltdown of a few years ago, people were buying homes for as little as 3 percent down, borrowing 97 percent of the home's price.

When you buy a commercial building, such as a block of apartments, you'll typically put 35 percent down, and the remaining 65 percent will be debt, structured in various ways. Some people can manage debt very well, but some can't. Debt isn't necessarily a bad thing, but if you own real estate you will have to work with it.

Real estate involves management and maintenance. When you own bonds, you usually put them away and wait for them to

mature. When you buy a stock, you sometimes have to watch the performance of the company that's represented by the stock, to be sure your investment isn't ruined. But if you own real estate, you have to be aware of it all the time.

You have to be sure it's leased, and that your tenants are paying their rent on time. You have to screen tenants; you might have to run credit checks on them. (You certainly will have to do that if it's a commercial tenant.) You have to deal with the tenants' complaints. You have to deal with it if the furnace quits or a pipe bursts at three in the morning. (Have you ever known these problems to present themselves at a convenient time?)

You have to keep the building clean, safe, and in good general shape so that tenants will want to keep renting from you. Yes, you can hire a management company to do all that for you, but then you have to watch the management company—because if they screw up, your investment's in trouble. And they can cost you anywhere up to 10 percent of your rents.

Bottom line: investing in stocks only requires money. Investing in real estate involves money, time, and sweat.

Real estate is physically vulnerable. It can get flooded, it can catch fire, it can be vandalized. Your tenants can damage it. It can also be physically seized by the bank if you can't pay off your loans, or by the courts if you don't pay your taxes. A publicly traded company sometimes suffers damage to its infrastructure, of course, but that damage is usually not enough to slow or halt the company's overall operations. (On the other hand, you can insure real estate. You can't insure a stock.)

Real estate exposes you to liability in ways that other investments don't. You're not going to get sued for owning a stock or a bond. But you certainly might be liable for personal injury if a tenant breaks his leg on your property because the treads on a staircase were worn down. A prospective tenant might sue you for some imagined discrimination, when in fact you turned him down

because of poor credit. The local government could cite and fine you for any number of code violations.

Real estate is like a mistress. You have to keep putting money into a building to keep it happy, and sometimes that means taking money out of your other investments, or dipping into your retirement account, or borrowing at unacceptably high interest. If you're not careful, you might become emotionally attached to the asset, and find that the building owns you, rather than vice versa. You seldom have that problem with a stock.

The Pluses

Real estate's value can be increased—by you. If you own an apartment building, you can improve it in any number of ways: landscaping, buying better appliances, adding services, upgrading units as they become vacant. You can take a run-down building and turn it into a gem. Can you wield that much influence over the performance and value of a company you own stock in? Not unless you're the CEO of that company.

Real estate gives you a feeling of control. It's a tangible asset; you can see it, touch it, and manage it. Its success is almost entirely in your hands. When you buy a stock, you're in effect lending money to the company that issued that stock, and you're trusting that company to pay you back with dividends and growth—but you're not in control of that company. You're also not in control of the stock market, which is volatile and subject to the whims of the market. A worrisome item in the news can sometimes send all stock prices tumbling. The value of your building is mostly up to you.

Real estate is a hedge against inflation. If you've chosen your property well, its value will appreciate in the long run, and that appreciation will take into account any inflation of the currency.

You can adjust the rents annually, if it's a residential building. The market value of the building might fluctuate depending on market conditions, but that won't matter if you're keeping it leased and collecting rents.

Real estate promises a strong return. If you've chosen your property wisely, you can realize a return of about 6 percent annually, as well as some tax breaks, which is much better than you'll do with a retirement account, or a savings account, or with many stocks.

Real estate gives you a lot of flexibility with regard to taxation. For example, by deducting the depreciation of the rental, you can report a loss on your taxes even if you made a profit. The government will get back that depreciation when you sell the property, at a tax rate of 25 percent, in addition to whatever capital gains tax you have to pay, but you might find that you're willing to make that tradeoff. Of course, if you keep that property for life, your heirs won't have to pay any capital gains tax, since they'll be inheriting the property at its current market value.

Real estate is fun. Some people get their kicks out of trading stocks, and I understand that. Some people enjoy collecting a slow, steady return on their investments, and spending their time on pursuits that don't make money. I get that, too. But being a real estate investor means being a gladiator in the arena. It means meeting, and working with, a lot of interesting and stimulating people. It means learning, every day. It means controlling your own destiny.

There's just nothing like it.

How to Invest in Real Estate

In effect, there are four basic types of real estate investment: debt or equity, public or private. **Private equity** is the simplest and most straightforward. That's when you have a direct ownership interest in a property. You can own real estate as sole proprietor, or you can

participate with other investors by purchasing real estate as part of a pool, or syndicate, with your return based on your share of the investment.

- **Private debt** is when you invest in real estate by lending money for the purchase of a property, or for development of new property, or improvement of existing property.
- **Public equity** involves investing in real estate stocks, such as REITs, or investing in publicly traded real estate services firms and operating companies.
- **Public debt** is created when real estate loans are bundled together in various ways and sold as securities. These can come in the form of residential or commercial mortgage-backed securities (MBS or CMBS), or a mortgage REIT: a REIT that owns real estate debt rather than actual bricks and mortar. There are also mutual funds that invest in REITs, CMBS, and MBS.

I'm involved in private equity—the owning and trading of buildings—and that's mainly what I'll talk about in this book.

Types of Commercial Real Estate

Commercial real estate is real estate that is used for business purposes, and invested in to make money—as opposed to residential real estate, such as your house.

Office

Office is the glamor category of real estate. Office property could be a dedicated single-tenant office building, a multitenant facility, or a mixed-use property of which office might be one component. Office includes anything from a one-story building in a small town to a skyscraper in a huge city.

Office properties are generally sorted into one of three classes:

- **Class A** properties are located in the best spots, are in the best condition, and offer the best amenities. Space in these buildings commands higher-than-average rent for the area—sometimes much higher—but the tenants also expect the absolute best service and maintenance at all times.

- **Class B** office buildings may be Class A properties that haven't been maintained in pristine condition, or that are just a little too old and outdated to be considered the top of the line; they could be in a little less prime of a location; or they may be new buildings that simply weren't built with the highest-quality materials, finishes, and amenities. These buildings are good, not great, and they command average rents. Class B buildings make solid investments because they can usually be transformed into Class A buildings without having to rebuild from scratch.

- **Class C** buildings could be Class B buildings that have gotten old and fallen into a disrepair, buildings in areas that don't attract many good tenants, or buildings that were simply never that good to begin with. They rent for less than the average for the area, and often have high turnover. You can sometimes find a gem hidden among Class C properties—an overlooked building that can be brought back to life (meaning bumped up to Class B) with some relatively simple renovation. But most investors looking at Class C properties are planning to tear them down and start from scratch.

There is no hard-and-fast rating system in place for office buildings. There's no organization handing out A, B, and C ratings like the health department hands them out to restaurants. The exact criteria for what makes a property an A, B, or C class building varies from city to city, and even neighborhood to neighborhood. This classification system is simply a good, widespread method

for ranking buildings that investors like to use as shorthand for determining their investment strategy.

Office buildings, especially Class A buildings, are usually priced too high to be owned by any but the wealthiest individuals, or by institutional investors or publicly traded companies. The nicest office buildings are high-profile—usually located in a central business district or a highly trafficked suburban location—so if you're an owner of office properties, you could easily become high-profile yourself.

It'll be in your best interests to publicize yourself, so as to attract attention to your buildings and make people want to rent space in them. If you're a major owner of office property, you'll probably be on TV and on the web quite frequently. The press will contact you for quotes. You'll probably want to hire a public relations company to create buzz and make you look good.

Owning offices is fun. It can also be risky. The performance of an office building—its occupancy rate, the rents it commands, its net income—is largely dependent on the economy, both nationally and locally. If the economy's strong, if there's demand for office workers in industries such as financial services, real estate services, insurance, and so on, office buildings will perform well. In an economic downturn, you're more likely to see tenants falling behind on their rent, or cutting back the amount of space they rent, or going out of business entirely and leaving you with vacancy.

In a situation like that, every owner suffers, but the owners of the best office properties usually suffer the least. In hard times, when vacancy is high, owners often have to lower their rents. This makes it easier for surviving businesses to take space in the Class A buildings. This means those businesses leave behind vacancies in the Class B buildings, forcing those owners to lower their rents to fill the space—and tenants from Class C buildings will also take advantage of the situation.

So, in a downturn, it's usually the Class C buildings that have the hardest time staying afloat. Keep in mind also that office buildings have very high operating costs. So, if you lose one of your bigger tenants, it's going to affect your net income pretty dramatically, because your operating costs don't care whether you're fully leased!

On the other hand, when the economy's good, if you have a Class A or Class B+ property, you can just about write your own ticket, because employers need space to put their workers, demand for quality space will be high, and it takes years for new buildings to come onto the market.

The economy also has great influence over the market value of office properties, and the Class B and C properties will suffer the most—because who wants to buy a building that already has a high vacancy?

Still, some investors specialize in Class B and C office properties and do quite well, in the long run. If you have the knack for it, and good business sense, you may find that these lower-rent properties are within your means and within your management capabilities.

Of all types of commercial real estate, office buildings are the properties that perform most like stocks. A well-located, perfectly maintained building in a big city is like a blue-chip stock: expensive to own, but it provides steady growth and steady income. Other office buildings are like speculative stocks. If the local economy is good, and if you give the building a lot of attention, it'll stay tenanted and bring you a lot of income. If the economy goes bad, or if a lot of new buildings come on the market, your building could suddenly lose tenants—and your remaining tenants might demand more favorable terms when their leases expire.

Office properties typically involve high potential returns and high risks, since an economic downturn can lead to vacancies and/or underperforming leases. Long lease terms usually translate to dependable cash flow, however.

Retail

Retail properties, a category that includes shopping malls, power centers (unenclosed shopping centers anchored by one or more big box store), and local strip malls, as well as individual store-fronts and standalone commercial buildings, depend on attracting credit tenants. A standalone bank branch, restaurant, gas station, or boutique shop would all be retail properties, as would giant grocery stores or enormous shopping plazas. Retail is an interesting category because it offers such variety of product, and so many different degrees of risk.

One type of retail property that's very popular with conservative investors is the "single-tenant net-leased" property. This is a standalone building, typically occupied by a retail tenant with extremely good credit, such as a drugstore, supermarket, or other chain retailer, on a lease of twenty years or more.

On a net lease, the tenant not only pays rent but takes responsibility for many of the owner's expenses: taxes, insurance, maintenance, repairs, and utilities. Various types of net leases exist, dividing the responsibilities in various ways. The most popular net lease is the triple net lease (the triple being taxes, insurance, and maintenance, in addition to rent and utilities). On a triple net lease, the tenant is virtually the owner of the building, with the true owner realizing a small return over a long term.

Your return on a single-tenant net-leased property will be small, but steady, and you'll be able to count on that steady income for a long time. If you want to just relax and cash the rent check every month, this is a great way to go. It's not my way, because I'm more of a hands-on guy. I want a bigger return on my investment, and I'm glad to work for it.

A strip center or a mall will typically have one big tenant, called the "anchor." The anchor of a strip center will usually be a supermarket; a mall will more usually have a department store as its anchor. A larger mall might have two anchor tenants, one on each end of the layout, such as a department store and a movie multiplex.

In some ways, retail is a lower-risk investment than office. For one thing, the leases tend to be longer-term and more likely to be renewed. (Retailers hate to relocate.) For another, the operating costs tend to be lower. For a third, if you choose your tenants wisely, a mall or strip center is less likely than an office building to be hurt by a bad economy. (No matter how bad the economy is, people still need to eat, and get their eyeglasses repaired—and when times are hard, people go to movies more often.)

Retail is interesting, but it's not my kind of investment. Retail might appeal to the mom-and-pop investor who owns a strip mall or shopping center in a suburban location, but owners of major malls and power centers tend to be very large, highly capitalized, publicly traded investors, such as Kimco and Brixmor. Neighborhood centers usually contain local businesses, while malls and power centers are more likely to attract national brands.

Industrial

Industrial real estate includes factories, research and development facilities, warehouses, logistics facilities, storage facilities, switching facilities, and much more. Medical facilities are often grouped in this category, although, depending on the type of operation, they might also be classified as retail or office properties.

Industrial is the category I know the least about, and I don't want to know much about it. Some investors find it interesting, and there's money to be made in it. You can have your choice of warehouses, self-storage buildings, call centers, factories, research and development facilities, and lots of other types of property within this broad category.

These properties tend to pretty much take care of themselves, so they're not too demanding on the owner, and the risk is usually low, but so is the return.

Industrial properties can be cheap to develop and operate, easy to maintain, and lease terms tend to be long. However, rents tend to be low, and dependent on economic growth. Hospitals and medical office likewise offer steady, low-risk returns, but with little excitement. Self-storage facilities generally can charge high rents, but short lease terms can cause vacancy issues.

You might compare industrial properties with bonds. They're often perceived as "defensive" investments.

Land

Land? In Brooklyn? Fuhgeddaboudit. While it's not as common in big, heavily developed cities, in some parts of the country investing in land makes good sense. This might be rural land that has never been developed and lies in the path of future development. It might be "greenfield" (undeveloped, or once-developed but now clean) land in an urban area, or "brownfield" land (previously developed, contaminated, and requiring environmental cleanup). Some investors prefer timberland: forested areas where mature trees can be cut down and used for building or other purposes, and new trees planted. They're not making any more land, so in general it will probably appreciate in value. But if you own land, you'll have to put it to use, which requires some sort of specialized knowledge, and usually some very hard work.

Hotel

Hotel property includes motels, country inns, big-city hotels, conference centers, resorts, and corporate retreats. Hotels was the area where I thought I might end up at one point. I mentioned earlier that I'd had the idea, as a teenager, of running several Airbnb-style hotels in Brooklyn. If I'd gotten to that market a little earlier, ahead of the big hotel chains that broke ground in the borough right around that same time, I might have ended up with a career as an owner and manager of hotels. Hotels are a feast-or-famine proposition. Your occupancy can change dramatically from day to day; so can your rents. Hotels are very labor-intensive; they require a lot of hands-on attention. You're very vulnerable to government regulation, and to litigation, such as personal injury suits.

Hotels are volatile and cyclical. Capital expenditures are high, but so are the opportunities for fast profit.

Multifamily

Multifamily is what I focus on. Multifamily real estate includes the development of anything from a two-family house to high-rise apartment buildings to be sold or rented, as well as the buying and trading of existing properties. It includes everything from luxury condos and rentals to student housing, to retirement facilities.

Apartment buildings are what I like best to work with, and to invest in—especially in New York City, where supply is always going to be short. People always need shelter, and not everyone can own a home—not everyone wants to—so there'll always be demand for apartments. Apartments are a safe investment because you'll seldom have significant vacancy. You might have an empty unit now and then, but you're not going to suddenly lose an anchor tenant and have 50 percent of the property unoccupied.

Multifamily is higher-risk, in some ways, than some other property types. Your tenants pay the rent, and most or all of their utilities (in most cases the landlord pays for water and sewage disposal), but the owner is responsible for taxes and insurance, and for all maintenance.

On the other hand, the apartment market is less cyclical than the office market. If anything, apartments will be a better investment if the economy overall isn't good—because people will be holding off on buying homes, and they'll rent apartments instead.

Apartment buildings, if you take good care of them, are bound to be money makers. They take a lot of time and attention, and tenants always have complaints. And those complaints tend to come to you between 5:00 PM and 9:00 AM, and on weekends. On the other hand, owning and managing apartments isn't all that complicated. Just about anyone can figure out how to do it.

Another nice thing about owning apartment buildings is that it gives you opportunities to improve your community. If you own attractive, well-managed, well-tenanted apartment buildings, you'll be able to command high rents. You'll attract a better class of people, and you'll encourage owners of neighboring buildings to compete for those tenants by making their buildings as nice as yours. If your neighborhood gets a reputation as a place where nice people live, you'll attract a better grade of retailers, to serve them.

The government will like you, too, for driving up property values and improving the tax base. Your property taxes will rise, of course, as your building becomes more valuable, but those taxes will go largely to fund public schools—and better schools will also attract a more desirable type of tenant.

In terms of the properties I own, I'm pretty well concentrated in New York City, mostly Brooklyn. That's a good policy, in my opinion, because it's easy for me to keep an eye on all my properties. But I also own properties outside the city, even in other countries. For an investor who's experienced in keeping properties well maintained and running smoothly, anywhere in the world that people want to live can be a potential opportunity in the making.

How Real Estate Fits into the Investment Picture

Real estate can be regarded as a hybrid investment: a combination of a stock and a bond, only you're investing in an entity that you control. Real estate tends to appreciate in value like a stock, and it has an income stream like a bond—and you're the boss of it.

Usually, your income from the property will be fairly steady. It'll go up or down a little, of course, depending on whether you had to spend a little more or a little less on maintaining the property in a given month. But as long as you keep the units rented, you can expect the building's performance to be fairly stable.

The market value of your property could change considerably, from year to year, depending on various conditions—but as long as you're not selling the building, its market value is only an opinion. The income from it is the reality!

This theoretical market value, by the way, is determined by what comparable buildings have sold for, recently, in your neighborhood. Therefore, it's an extremely inaccurate way of determining what your building is worth.

For example, suppose you bought your building a few years ago for $800,000. Because of improvements you've made, plus a little inflation, you figure you should get $1 million for it. But suppose sales in your neighborhood have been slow in the past few months. The building next door to yours, which is about the same size and about as nice, did recently sell for $1 million. But the owner of the building next to it—a building that's also about the same size as yours, and about as nice—was in financial trouble and had to sell at a loss. He only got $700,000 for his property. Therefore, all else being equal, an appraiser might say that the market value of your property would be $850,000: the average of the sale prices of those two comparable properties.

That's why property owners hate it when a neighboring owner has to sell at a loss: It drives down the theoretical market value of their properties. As you can imagine, it's especially damaging if the bank forecloses on a property near you, because it's certain to be sold for *far* less than its market value.

If you've done your research on recent sales, and find that based on them, the market value of your property is much less than what you believe it's worth, you might not want to try to sell it— because buyers will look at those comparables, and they'll come in with a lowball figure and insist that the building isn't worth what you say it is. In that case, hang onto it. As in the rest of life, don't sell yourself short!

A Basic Investment Plan

If you're going to invest in real estate—and for the sake of this discussion, let's say you're going to invest in apartment buildings— you'll need to think about where you'll own, and how you'll grow your portfolio. I'd advise you to follow several guidelines.

First, as I advised before, stay in one geographical area. Ideally,

you should be able to drive to any of your properties in thirty minutes. Second, stick to one type of real estate, rather than buying apartment buildings, offices, industrial parks, farms, and so on. Different property types call for different types of expertise.

Third, either manage the properties yourself or get a highly regarded management company to do it for you. Don't just hire a super and hope for the best.

Fourth, put as much equity into your properties as you can. Too much leverage—debt, in other words—is a recipe for disaster. Of course you'll have some debt, but keep it as low as you can afford—and don't add more properties if they're going to put you in a deep hole. I'll discuss debt in greater depth later in this book.

Fifth, avoid partnerships on a given investment if you can. If you have to take on another investor as a partner, make sure that you're the senior partner, and do your best to buy your partner out as soon as possible. Partnerships are a common and necessary part of business, but there are just so many ways for even the most stable-seeming partnership to go south when it comes to property investment. I've seen partnerships fall apart over something as simple as deciding which light fixtures to use for a renovation. If you can afford to invest solo, that will allow you to call all the shots and spare you some future headaches.

• • •

Some investors—like me—use a flexible strategy for portfolio growth. They'll seize whatever opportunity looks good to them. If the right property becomes available in the right neighborhood, at any time, they'll jump on it. This strategy works for some investors, but if that's the way you're going to grow, you need to do it with your eyes wide open. You need to be aware of the hazards.

Growing too fast is probably the biggest danger, with this strategy. If you accumulate more property than you can manage, or more debt than you can easily pay, you'll be in trouble. You might end up having to sell some of your property to pay off that debt, and in the worst case you'll be left with nothing.

A more conservative, patient investor will set a timetable for growth. One popular strategy is to try to double the size of your portfolio at regular intervals, depending on your ability to raise capital. You might start by buying one apartment building, putting in as much equity as you can, and keeping your leverage low. After you've paid down the debt for five years or so, you can refinance, freeing up enough capital to make a down payment on another property. Then you repeat the process.

In another five years, you'll be able to refinance both those properties, which will give you enough capital to buy two more buildings. Five years after that, you can buy four more—and in twenty years, if you stick to the schedule, you'll have accumulated fifteen buildings, which is a nice little empire.

Of course, you probably won't grow at such a precise rate. You might find that it doesn't make sense to buy anything at the end of a five-year period, or you might find some irresistible opportunity that can't wait. But many investors do try to keep a certain schedule of growth in mind.

Real estate transactions tend to be long and costly, for both the buyer and the seller. Various brokerage fees are usually involved. The lender will charge fees in addition to the interest on the loan. Unless you're in an unusually hot market cycle, it'll take some time to find a buyer at the price you want, and unless it's a very slow market you shouldn't expect to find any bargains, if you're the buyer.

For those reasons, most experts say you shouldn't "time the market." That is, you shouldn't make your decisions on when to sell or buy based on where you think the market is going. Make your move at a time that fits your overall strategy, taking into account the current market conditions and asking yourself whether it makes sense to go ahead with your original plans.

Probably the key is to ask yourself, "How much risk am I comfortable with? How patient am I?" There's nothing wrong with taking a calculated risk, and there's nothing wrong with playing safe. It's a matter of knowing your objectives and your personality.

This is another reason to love real estate: it's so flexible. Real estate doesn't mature, like a bond. You can draw up and execute a business plan for a building, or a portfolio of buildings, based on any timetable you like, whether you intend to flip the building in a year or keep it to leave to your heirs.

• • •

Don't expect to make big money right away. Most investors advise you to keep your rents reasonably low to attract tenants quickly. You don't want to sell yourself short by dramatically underpricing the market, but don't try to go higher than the average rent in the area unless you're positive that your property really offers significantly more than your nearby competitors. The consensus is that on an apartment building, you should charge enough rent to cover your mortgage and other costs, and ideally make a net return of about one percent of the building's value. Later, when your mortgage is paid off, naturally your return will be much higher.

If you've chosen your property wisely and maintained it well, its value will inevitably appreciate over the long term. As you've probably noticed, the national economy runs in cycles, with growth followed by occasional recessions, which are fairly predictable. Real estate works the same way, with property values and rents gradually going up, then cycling down for a couple of years, followed by another cycle of growth. So, your property might lose value, on paper, from time to time. (Real estate values tend to "lag the economy," so to speak, so values will usually drop a few months after the national economy turns down, and rise after the economy has been in recovery for a while.) Don't worry. Just hold onto your property, and wait for it to start appreciating again.

Most investors use a "buy and hold" strategy. They'll buy a property and keep it for years as they gradually buy another property and another, slowly growing their portfolio. They'll sell a property from time to time, but always as part of an ongoing strategy. A successful buy-and-hold investor will have a well-considered plan for growth, and a pretty good idea of how long he'll hold a property.

"Flippers" are the opposite type of investor. They're gamblers, looking to make a series of fast, small gains. They'll watch the market, buy when prices are low, and hold onto the building just until the market turns up, when they can sell at a profit. These are opportunistic investors, who look for properties that are undervalued, or that are located in neighborhoods that are about to gentrify. Flippers usually won't spend much time or money on improving the property.

You can make a lot of money this way, in the long run—if you know what you're doing. But it's risky. Typically, a flipper operates on an all-cash basis. He doesn't borrow. So, if he's not able to sell the property at a profit, within a certain time frame, he's going to be in big trouble. He'll have to sell at a loss, sometimes at a catastrophic loss. Thus, successful flippers have to be very knowledgeable of how the market works, and they have to be able to react quickly to shifting circumstances.

Another type of flipper is the investor who holds a property long enough to add value to it through renovations and other improvements. This is usually less risky. You usually will be able to get financing for a deal like this, and you're almost certain to sell at a profit. The drawback to this strategy is that it's slow money, since you'll usually only be able to handle one or two properties at a time. It's also a lot of work. But if renovation is your hobby, it can be great fun.

Alternatives to Buying Property

If you want to invest in real estate, but don't have enough capital to buy a property on your own, you'll still find other ways to start a modest portfolio, and build it—and eventually you'll be able to afford a building or two of your own.

You might invest in a mutual fund that concentrates on owning real estate. Or you might consider joining a real estate investment group. There are vehicles by which you can own one or more units within a block of apartments, or perhaps the group buys or develops a building or several buildings, which are collectively managed. As with mutual funds, the risk is diluted—but your earnings can be diluted by management fees. In an arrangement like this, if you own specific units, and they're vacant, your mortgage will be paid through a pool formed by all owners to safeguard against this eventuality.

Another popular alternative to owning a property outright is buying shares in a real estate investment trusts (REIT). REITs provide an easy and low-risk way to get into the game. These are companies that own and operate commercial real estate. Sometimes they own real estate debt as well. They finance their operation through the sale of stock in their company—stock that might or might not be publicly traded. They're vehicles by which investors can, in effect, own real estate without buying an entire property. While there's considerable variation among REITs as to what they own, how they're managed, and their overall strategies, REITs are generally regarded as sound investments for several reasons. These include:

- **Diversification.** REITs own multiple properties over a considerable geographical area, so their risk is spread out.
- **Dividends.** Most REITs are regarded as income stocks rather than growth stocks. That is, they usually produce a dependable dividend (with which, of course, investors can buy more shares if they choose), although the value of the shares might not grow dramatically.
- **Inflation protection.** Because REITs can usually build inflation into the rents they charge on their properties, their earnings and net asset value tend not to be diluted by currency inflation.

* **Long-term performance.** As opposed to many other stocks, which depend on the performance of the company's business, REIT stocks depend on the performance of the company's assets. REITs' underlying assets are land and buildings, which have intrinsic value and cash flows tied to legally binding leases.

* **Transparency.** Because most REITs are publicly traded and their assets (the real estate) are tangible, it's easy for an investor to assess a REIT's performance and make an informed decision to buy, hold, or sell.

By law, REITs pay out at least 90 percent of their taxable income as dividends. Almost all REITs specialize in owning one property type or another: offices, hotels, medical facilities, shopping malls, and so on. Other REITs invest in timberland, prisons, or debt on commercial or residential property. REITs offer varying risks and varying returns. You might also consider putting your money into a mutual fund that invests in many different REITs.

REITs vary widely in terms of their investment strategy. Some are more speculative than others; some are more highly leveraged than others. Structures vary dramatically, too. On the whole, though, the structure, strategy, and performance of an REIT are easy for its investors to follow.

The bottom line is, a stock and a building are both capable of earning or losing money. A bad guess on either type of investment could force you to sell at a loss. In both cases, though, if you choose wisely, your chances of a loss are slim.

Both a Borrower and a Lender Be

Let me tell you a little about equity and debt, and how they both relate to building a real estate portfolio. If you're going to be a real estate entrepreneur, you're going to have to deal with debt—and probably a lot of debt—unless you're already wealthy and able to pay for everything with cash—which you're not, right?

A hundred years ago, if you wanted to buy a building, you generally had to put down half of the building's price. The rest you'd typically pay off over seven years. This meant that it was very difficult for most people to own their own homes, let alone apartment buildings, hotels, or office properties. Starting in the 1930s, for various reasons, it became somewhat easier for an ordinary family to own a home. By the 1950s it was possible for a working-class family to pay off a mortgage over thirty years. Home ownership became commonplace in most of the United States. But it was still very hard to own commercial real estate without making a substantial down payment, which very few individuals could do. Thus, commercial buildings tended to be owned by institutions— insurance companies, pension funds, and so on—or by a few very wealthy families.

Even if you had the money, it was very risky to invest in commercial property, because you'd have all your capital tied up in it. If you had trouble keeping the building leased, you'd have a cash flow problem, and the sale value of the building would decline. So, individuals hardly ever bought commercial buildings in the old days.

Then, in the 1950s, an entrepreneur named William Zeckendorf came up with the idea of buying buildings using more debt and less equity. Zeckendorf was able to do this by getting several different lenders to put money into the property—creating several layers of debt, so to speak—while investing very little of his own money. By investing in this way, you create relatively little risk for yourself. In the worst case, if you can't pay your creditors, they'll take over the building, but since you didn't have much of your own money tied up in it, that won't be so terrible.

Zeckendorf used to say, "If I owe you $100,000, and I can't pay, I'm in trouble. If I owe you $100 million, and I can't pay, *you're* in trouble!" What he meant was that if you're going to go into debt, do it in such a way that your lenders can't afford to let you fail.

Of course, if the lenders know that you're so highly leveraged, they'll charge you a higher interest rate. The more risk they're taking, the more they'll want to be paid for it. So, in order to justify the cost of the loans, you're going to have to run your building really well, to be sure it makes money. In effect, the more you borrow, the more you're betting on your own ability to operate your property.

• • •

A mortgage is a lien, or a claim, on your property by whatever person or institution has lent you the money to pay for it. Under the terms of the mortgage, you pay off the loan via a predetermined set of payments, over a set period (usually many years). The property you've purchased is a pledge of your good faith. If you default on payments, the lender can foreclose on the mortgage; that is, take possession of the building and sell it to settle the remaining debt.

Most economists call a mortgage "good debt." You're building equity in the property as you pay it off, and it protects you from having too much actual cash tied up in the property. Also, once you've paid down some of that debt, you can continue to borrow against that property and use the second and third mortgages to buy other buildings. This can be an effective strategy whether you're a buy-and-hold investor or a flipper—although it's typically difficult for a flipper to raise debt capital.

If you're using this strategy, you're almost certainly going to depend on cash flow from your properties to pay off those mortgages. This means keeping your properties well maintained, so you don't have to spend much on repairs; it also means ensuring that the properties are fully leased to tenants who pay the rent on time, every month.

Debt is like alcohol. In moderation, it's good for you. If you borrow only what you can afford, at a favorable interest rate, you can invest that borrowed money in such a way that it'll earn more than your debt service. (For example, you might borrow $1 million, at an annual debt service of $60,000, to buy a building that will bring you a net income of $75,000.)

Most homeowners don't buy their homes in cash; they take out a mortgage. This, too, is considered good debt, because you build equity in your house, over the years, rather than renting your house and simply handing your money over to the landlord every month. Moreover, the interest on a real estate loan—whether it's for your own home or for an investment property—is usually low compared to other types of debt.

Bad debt is credit card debt, or a payday loan, or any debt you've taken on something you don't need. (Many homeowners lose their homes in an economic downturn because they bought a bigger, more expensive house than they needed, with too small of a down payment.)

As an investor in real estate, you'll almost always carry some debt—but you want to keep that debt low enough, and simple enough, that you can manage it. When Donald Trump talks about being "the king of debt," that's because he follows Zeckendorf's high-debt strategy. Investors like him will put together deals that involve many layers of debt, many different lenders. They might take in equity partners as well.

But not every investor is properly equipped to operate that way. Trump can do it because he has a terrific staff behind him. He's got highly trained people in his organization, who know how to keep track of his transactions, make sure everything's legal, and see to it that everybody gets paid on schedule. But if you're just one person, or one person with a small staff, you're going to want to avoid complications. You'll want your mortgages as uncomplicated as possible, and you'll want to work with just a few lenders whom you know are reliable.

If it's possible—and it isn't, always—you'll want to borrow from a lender who won't sell your mortgage to another party. If you have a personal relationship with whoever is holding your mortgage, you'll find it easier to work with him—if, for example, you're temporarily having trouble with the payments, or if you want to renegotiate the debt to cover some improvements you want to make on the property.

If your original lender has sold the note, you never know who you'll have to deal with when it's time to refinance, or if any difficulties arise. Your mortgage might even have been chopped up into different pieces and securitized—sold like a stock—so that it won't be owned by any one person.

If your lender does sell your loan, always find out who is in control of it. Be sure there's one person you can contact with any questions or problems, and develop a good relationship with that person.

• • •

You'll be a borrower, when you invest in real estate. But you'll also, in effect, be a lender.

Any time you invest, think of it in terms of lending money. When you lend money to another person, you're doing it on the assumption that you'll be paid back, with interest. You're not lending to be nice; you're lending to make money. You'll consider your loan an investment. That's why you'll run a credit check on the person you're lending to (at least I sure hope you will!) and otherwise satisfy yourself that the borrower is not going to default on the loan. You're aware of the interest rate of the loan, and the term of the loan, and thus you know how much money you're likely to make, and when you'll be done with that investment.

It's the same thing when you buy a stock. When you buy a stock, you're lending money to the company whose stock you're buying. So, you look at that company's financials. You look at its annual reports; you look at its past performances; you get as clear an idea as possible of how that company is likely to perform over the next few years.

You look at your anticipated return: dividends, plus likely appreciation of the stock price.

You also look at your exit strategy. How long are you likely to

hold onto the stock? Will it be part of your portfolio indefinitely, or do you plan to sell it in X number of years, or when its price hits a certain level?

A person who's doing well can usually borrow quite a lot of money. That's why a rich man can buy a nice big house. He'll still have a mortgage, but lenders are glad to give him a large loan at a favorable rate because they see it as a good investment. A poor man might not be able to qualify for anything more than a payday loan—a small loan at a high interest rate—because the risk to the lender is much higher.

A business that's seen as strong and growing, likewise, will command a high stock price, while a company that nobody has heard of, that has no track record, might be only a "penny stock." Again, it's about the risk to the investor. (If you're a day trader, you're not so much an investor as you are a gambler, which is fine, but that's not the subject of this book.)

With a building, you're likewise taking a big risk if you buy a run-down building in a seedy neighborhood—so the price of the building should be low. Here's what makes this investment more attractive than a high-risk personal loan or the purchase of a high-risk stock: *You control the asset.*

When you buy a building, even if you're borrowing money to buy it, you have to think of it in terms of lending money to the building. How likely is it that the building will justify your investment? Is it well located? Is the character of the neighborhood likely to change, for the better or the worse? Is the building fully tenanted by people who can be depended on to pay the rent? In other words, is that building a good risk?

PART 5

Making Money in Real Estate

You make money off your investment properties in two ways: income and appreciation. Income is simply the rents and fees you collect from your tenants, minus the expenses of operating the property, taxes, and service on your debt. Appreciation is the increase in the market value of the property over time. You can realize income as long as you own the property, but you can't realize appreciation unless you sell or refinance the property.

You can cause a property to appreciate by improving it. For example, if you own a piece of land, you might increase its value by building a house on it, or by turning it into a farm, or subdividing it into multiple smaller lots that can be used to bring in multiple revenue streams. If you own a building, you can improve it so as to attract tenants who'll pay a higher rent.

You can also cause your property to appreciate by improving the surrounding area. You might join a neighborhood association to make the neighborhood cleaner and safer; you might lobby the city government to improve the surrounding infrastructure, thus attracting more businesses to serve your tenants.

A property can also appreciate due to inflation. As prices rise generally, the market value of the property will rise—but appreciation caused by inflation is canceled out by the fact that other goods and services will have also gone up in price.

• • •

Before you make your first move as a real estate investor, ask yourself why you're doing it. Obviously, you're doing it to make money, but to what end? Are you investing for the long term, so that you'll be able to sell the assets when you retire? Are you investing with the goal of building a large portfolio of properties, so that eventually you can live off the income from them? Are you buying properties with the intention of selling them at a profit as soon as you can?

Your "why" will inform your what, your when, your where, and your how, as you put together your investment strategy and your management strategy.

You should also ask yourself, "What needs can I fill by investing in real estate?" Does your community need apartments? Then buy an old apartment building, renovate it, and make it more attractive—or buy a big townhouse and turn it into rental units. Is your community under-retailed? Then maybe you could find some vacant land where you could develop a strip center. Has there been a rash of foreclosures in your community? Then work with lenders to see if you can take some of the foreclosed property off their hands.

The bottom line is, a successful business almost always depends on filling a need. If you can solve someone else's problems by investing in real estate, you'll probably be successful. When you've determined what your goal is, and what the local needs are, you'll have an idea of what kind of investor you should be. Then choose a specialty—whether it's apartments, retail, development, or brokerage—and get really good at it.

If you know your goals as an investor, and you know your long-term strategy, you'll find it easier to evaluate the merits of a deal. Say you're thinking about buying a certain property, and you want to know whether or not it's the right buy for you. Let's say, for example, that you've decided to specialize in buying distressed properties, fixing them up, and selling them at a profit. Every time you look at a property, you should have a minimum profit in mind.

That is, as part of your strategy, you might say to yourself, "I'm not going to buy any building that I'm not sure I can sell at a profit of at least $50,000."

If you hold yourself to that strict standard—passing on any deal that doesn't meet that standard—you will make money on every deal. Sure, now and then you'll guess wrong, and you'll end up having to sell at a profit of less than $50,000, but you'll never be so far wrong that you'll lose money on the deal. And sometimes you'll sell the asset for a profit much greater than $50,000.

You can use the same sort of thinking if you're pursuing a buy-and-hold strategy. If you're buying apartment buildings with the idea of keeping them indefinitely, set yourself a certain minimum anticipated cash flow, and refuse to look at any building that won't provide it.

Always look for what we call "motivated sellers": owners who have a good reason to sell the building. Don't spend too much time dealing with owners who don't need to sell—but stay on good terms with them, because one day they might become more motivated than they are now!

• • •

If you don't have capital to invest right now, and if you're not making enough money to set anything aside for later investment, I'd advise you to find a job, or start a business, that is somehow related to real estate. If you have the personality and the drive for it, sales and brokerage might be for you—and the industry is always looking for brokers who are PSD: poor, smart, and driven. If that kind of life doesn't appeal to you, you might try landscaping, carpentry, or construction. You might even consider starting a maid service. That's a good way to meet property owners, learn about property, and learn about the markets—and you'll usually be one of the first to know if a property goes on sale.

• • •

Whatever type of real estate you're investing in, the capitalization rate—cap rate, for short—will be a vital piece of information. You should be able to calculate a cap rate in your head, or at least with pen and paper, almost without thinking about it. And once you're used to the concept, you'll be able to do just that. Figuring the cap rate on a building becomes as automatic as figuring the tip on a restaurant bill.

Your cash-on-cash return—the money you get out of your investment compared to your down payment—is a very important performance metric for most real estate assets. If you buy a building at a price of $1 million, putting $250,000 down and borrowing the rest, and your net annual income from the building is $50,000, then you divide the income by your down payment to determine your cash-on-cash return. In this example, it's 20 percent.

Your cap rate is what your cash-on-cash return would be if you'd paid for the whole building in cash, borrowing nothing. In other words, you'd divide that $50,000 by the total price of $1 million, giving you a cap rate of 5 percent. (Usually, in the industry, you leave off the percent when you're talking about a cap rate, so you'll say "I bought the building at a five cap.") The cap rate is analogous to a stock's price-to-earnings ratio.

In the market, the cap rate of a building is usually tied to its risk. You might be happy to buy a building at only a four cap if it were an absolutely solid asset that you knew would be fully leased for a long time and was unlikely to incur any unforeseen expenses. But if it were a more speculative investment, one where you were taking a lot of risk, you'd want to buy it at a much higher cap rate.

If you're looking at an apartment building, you'll look at the income that that property is making right now, and compare it with the incomes from other, similar properties in the neighborhood. You'll determine the level of risk you'll be taking, if you buy that building, and you'll offer to buy it at a cap rate that pays you for your risk and gives you the return you require.

To determine a building's cap rate, start by figuring its net operating income (NOI) for the past twelve months. This includes

not just the rents from tenants but any extra fees and rents for parking, cleaning services, and so on.

Then, determine total expenses for the past twelve months. These would include whatever you spent on maintenance and repairs, advertising, insurance, taxes, garbage removal, and any utilities that the tenant wasn't responsible for. (The landlord usually pays for water and sewage.) Then, simply subtract those expenses from your gross income, and you have your NOI.

Suppose that's $50,000, and the owner of the property is offering to sell it to you for $1 million. Just divide the NOI by his asking price, and you'll see that you'd be buying at a five cap.

You might find that other buildings in the neighborhood are performing at about that level, and you might decide that a five cap, on that particular building, is consistent with your investment strategy. In that case, go ahead and buy. More likely, though, you'll find that the owner is pricing his building a little higher than it's worth. And you might be hoping, in any case, to buy a building at a 6.5 cap—but you'll settle for a 6. So, to determine what you'd pay for that building to get a 6.5 cap rate, you divide that $50,000 by 6.5, and add two zeros to that number, and you get $769,230. Fine. Offer the owner $770,000 and see if he bites. He probably won't, but that's just your first offer. Maybe let him talk you up to $830,000—a six cap—and call it a deal.

On the other hand, maybe other buildings in that neighborhood are performing at a five cap level, but your owner is offering the building at a six cap. In that case, you've probably met one of those "motivated sellers" we've talked about.

• • •

Unless you're living at the bottom of the Grand Canyon, real estate deals are nearby, no matter where you are. It's just a matter of finding them, weeding out the ones you don't want, and zeroing in on those that make sense in relation to your objectives and your

strategy. I can think of seven terrific sources right off the bat that anyone can access.

1. **Shoe leather.** Politicians call it "walking your precinct." Just choose an area of a few city blocks, every day, and walk around it, taking note of properties that are for sale—and properties you wish were for sale. But don't just be looking to buy. Get a feel for the neighborhood. Take note of who the main owners are. Talk to people here and there: the local retailers, or the building supers if they're out sweeping the sidewalk. Introduce yourself to people's dogs, and get the person on the other end of the leash to tell you a little about the neighborhood, what he likes and doesn't like about it, and what changes he's seen lately. Bring your business cards with you, and exchange them with local businesspeople. Bring a notebook.

2. **Real estate listing sites.** You'd be crazy not to use all the sites that exist now as a resource. From Zillow, Trulia, LoopNet, and services like CoStar, people find deals online all the time, but don't just use them to find deals for yourself. For example, if you spend some time on a site like LoopNet every day, you'll get a feeling for how markets are shaping up, in your region and all over the world. It'll put you in touch with a huge network of owners and brokers, and you can start building your network even if you're not immediately looking to buy or sell.

3. **Social media.** I'm a big user of social media every day. Being active on Facebook or Instagram doesn't get me a lot of deals directly, and it probably won't get you many, either, but it's a great way to remind people that you're out there—and it's a great way to attract people you might otherwise never have met. When people see what I'm up to on Facebook, SnapChat, or Twitter,

they might say, "Hey, that kind of life looks good to me!" and I might have them calling me about setting up another Rapid Realty franchise. Or, if they're looking for an apartment and they keep seeing me on social media, they might think to call the nearest Rapid Realty office.

4. **Direct mail.** You can't expect a high response rate from direct mail. If you send letters to every building owner in a neighborhood, one out of every hundred might get back to you, if you've sent a strong, compelling letter. You can get, from your county courthouse, a list of all rental property owners. Make a list of all those who own buildings that fall within your comfort zone— such as apartment buildings with at least X number of units. Of the few who call you, most will not be very interested in selling, and will quote you an unacceptable price. But at least you're on each other's radars.

5. **Banks.** I've said it before and I'll say it again: Banks hate owning real estate. If you've decided to focus on distressed assets, you have *got* to have good connections with all your local banks. But even if you're looking for healthy assets, banks are your friends. For one thing, banks often manage the assets of high-net-worth individuals—and those people usually own real estate. You never know when one of them might want to sell a property, and if the asset manager knows who you are, you might get the first call.

6. **The county sheriff.** In most jurisdictions, the sheriff and his deputies are in charge of serving eviction notices and other unpleasant news. They'll always have connections to landlords—and if they're landlords with deadbeat tenants, they'll probably be pissed-off landlords, and quite responsive to your suggestion that they might want to sell their buildings to you! (Plus,

no matter where you are in the world, it never hurts to have the county sheriff for a good buddy.)

7. **CCIM.** A Certified Commercial Investment Member (CCIM) is a real estate professional who has earned that designation. The fraternity of CCIMs includes brokers, leasing professionals, investment counselors, asset managers, appraisers, corporate real estate executives, property managers, developers, institutional investors, commercial lenders, attorneys, bankers, and other related professionals. The CCIM website provides an amazing wealth of information and connections—and deals. You might want to consider putting in the work required to earn the CCIM designation yourself.

PART 6

Your First Apartment Building

Finding the Right Property

Many investors enter the real estate game by buying a multifamily residential or mixed-use property. Beginning with just two to four units is a great way to start. That's what I did, and many of the buildings I bought after that first one stuck to that model as well. If you want to go bigger right off the bat, you might look at a building with eight to twenty units, but make sure you have good help in your corner before you take on a challenge of that size. Here are some tips to keep in mind when you're looking for your first apartment building.

As with just about any other type of property, the three secrets to buying the right apartment building are location, location, and location. The neighborhood in which your property's located will make all the difference in terms of what you pay for it and how you manage the asset.

Your property doesn't necessarily have to be located in a terrific neighborhood. Many investors recommend a strategy of buying not-so-great buildings in the best neighborhoods, and improving the buildings to drive up the rent. That's a very good idea, but it's not the only way to turn a profit.

Terrific neighborhoods—those with the best schools, the best

infrastructure, the best access to retail, and the highest per-family incomes—aren't always the best locations for a rental property, because they tend to attract buyers, not renters. A neighborhood that's not the fanciest—a neighborhood that's good, not great—is usually a more suitable location for rental properties.

A neighborhood where the schools, infrastructure, houses, and family incomes are a little above average is a great place to own property because a neighborhood like that will be what marketers call "aspirational." People who live there will be striving to improve themselves and their surroundings. They'll welcome a responsible landlord who is also interested in improving the community and who will bring respectable tenants into his building.

Even a neighborhood with a bad reputation—one with low incomes, higher crime rates, and a transient population—can be an advantageous place to own an apartment building. You won't have to worry about demand, because someone is always looking for lower-cost housing. But if you own in a bad neighborhood, you'll have to give your building a lot of attention, maybe even more than you'd give a building in the best neighborhood. You can do very well by owning a good building in a bad neighborhood. People will want to live in it, and will pay a premium rent—and by owning a safe, well-run building, you'll have a ripple effect on the surrounding area, so that in a few years, that bad neighborhood will have become a good one.

You need to pay attention not just to the property, and not just to the quality of the neighborhood. You also have to know how the neighborhood has been zoned by the local government. If you have a notion to turn the lower floors into retail and office space, for example, you had better know, before you buy, whether the zoning laws will permit it.

Get as much of your financing in place as you can before you start looking at properties and making offers. You won't be able to borrow money until you have a specific property in mind to buy, but you can visit several lenders beforehand, tell them what you're planning to do, show them all your financial information, and get an idea of how much you'll be able to borrow, on what terms.

Work with a broker. If you try to make the deal yourself, unless you are a trained real estate professional yourself, you'll be at a tremendous disadvantage: a street brawler against a guy who's got black belts in karate and aikido.

Interview several brokers, and avoid working with close friends or family. If you're working with a real estate agent to find a suitable property, avoid working with seller's agents. They'll have a fiduciary duty to the seller. However, it pays to talk to seller's agents, because they can point you to likely properties. It's often a good idea to work with a broker who is a Realtor—a member of the National Association of Realtors. Realtors have a pretty strong code of ethics that's meant to ensure that they'll look after the best interests of all parties to a deal. It's not a must to work with a Realtor—there are plenty of good brokers out there that may not be part of NAR, but it's an option.

Do your own research when you're looking at a building. Walk the neighborhood; question the locals. Look on the web to get an idea of what buildings are selling for in the area, on a per-square-foot basis, so that you'll know what to offer. Find out whether the building you're looking at has been on the market long, or whether it's been offered for sale by owner, or listed with some other brokerage. (If the answer to any of those questions is yes, you might be able to buy it for less than the asking price.)

Don't simply consider the price of the building. When you're negotiating with the seller, look for concessions. Would the seller be willing to make certain improvements prior to the sale? Would he assume the closing costs? Always look for these "value adds."

It's usually best to have more than one property in mind. If you get too emotionally attached to the idea of buying a particular property—well, it's like being obsessed with one particular girl. If you don't keep your options open…well, you know the rest.

Find out everything that's wrong with the building, and I mean everything. It's usually okay to buy a property that needs a little fixing—just so long as you know, going in, what needs to be done and how much it'll cost to do it. Many, many investors have bought a building that they thought was a bargain—and then they found out the hard way why it was priced so low.

Before you buy, determine whether you'll manage the property yourself or hire a management company. Unless you're a talented handyman and want to spend a lot of your time on the property, I'd recommend hiring a manager. They usually are not expensive— and the good ones are worth every penny.

When you're choosing a management company, of course you should ask other landlords for recommendations. But be careful not to put too much faith in what tenants say about a management company. Tenants just don't like building managers! After all, those are the people who collect the rent, and who hold back some of the deposit if the tenant has damaged the unit.

Are you going to live in the building? If you are, you might be able to get better terms on your mortgage—if you figure in the amount you'll be saving on rent. Tenants usually prefer a building that has the landlord on-premises. (The downside is that you'll get the first call when something goes wrong in the middle of the night.)

Whether or not you'll be managing the building yourself, get to know the tenants. Find out from the current owner if any of them are likely to give you problems in terms of paying rent on time, making noise, making unreasonable demands, not taking care of their unit, or abusing the common areas. The eviction process is long and costly, so do your best to prevent it ever happening. (And for heaven's sake, don't buy an empty building unless you're experienced at bringing in tenants. Even if it's a good deal, the building will do you no good if it doesn't produce a positive cash flow.)

Ownership and Management

Owning and managing a building is a science, not an art. It's a fairly simple science. If you're responsible and hardworking, and if you have normal intelligence, you can do it very well. Here are some pointers:

Don't overextend yourself. If you own a building of fewer than ten units, you can probably take care of all the maintenance and management yourself, if you want to. Much more than that, though, and you'll have to hire people, such as a building superintendent and maybe a cleaning company.

Don't scrimp on the hired help. Don't hire just anybody as maintenance or management personnel and pay them minimum wage. Hire experienced, knowledgeable people and pay them a market wage or salary. You get what you pay for, and if you're paying someone to manage your fortune—which you're doing, in this case—pay them well.

House rules should of course be included in the lease agreement—but post them in a prominent place in a public area of the building, too. These rules should include:

- Tenants are responsible for keeping a clean, orderly apartment. They will be held responsible for any damages caused by neglect or abuse of the unit, aside from ordinary wear and tear.
- Please tell the super immediately about any water leaks, wiring problems, mold, fire hazards, or vermin.
- Any alterations to the property must be approved in writing by the management.
- Management will make every effort to any problems with plumbing, heating, or physical damage (such as a broken window) within twenty-four hours.

You'll deal with contractors quite often in your career as a property owner. Whether it's a plumber, electrician, landscaper, carpenter, or generalist, you'll find that several basic rules apply.

First, do your homework. Before you hire a contractor, check its reputation with your local chamber of commerce, and get recent references. Look up the company on the web. (But don't automatically eliminate any candidate that has a few complaints against it on the web. Disgruntled customers are much more likely to comment than happy ones, and their complaints aren't always reasonable.)

Don't let a contractor pressure you with an offer that's "good for today only." Any reasonable contractor will give you at least a day to make up your mind. A contractor might ask for money up front, especially if it's a big project, and that's a fair request, but it shouldn't be the whole price of the project. Typically, you'll pay one-fourth to one-third of the estimated cost before any work is done, with more payments as the project progresses. Keep a paper trail of all agreements and payments.

Think about how you plan on collecting the rent from your tenants. If you're going to be living in the building (or if you have a property manager living in the building), you could always go with the time-tested "slip it under my door on the first of the month" method. This is as simple, low-cost, and low-tech as it gets. But it also means that when someone is late with the rent, they may go out of their way to avoid you and your apartment, creating an adversarial relationship between you. Not only does this create an unpleasant living situation, a tenant who's avoiding you because they owe you money is also not about to call you up if there's something wrong with their apartment, meaning that things could be breaking in their unit and you don't know about it. This could lead to a costly or even hazardous surprise down the road.

Another option is to have your tenants mail you the rent each month. Again, this is simple and cost-efficient—all it takes is an envelope and a stamp. But this method also gives delinquent tenants access to the oldest excuse in the book for late or missing rent payments: "It got lost in the mail."

These days, I prefer to have my tenants pay electronically. There are plenty of services out there that handle online rent payment. There are a couple major advantages to using an online service. Tenants can set up automatic monthly payments so that they don't have to remember to pay every month, which gives both you and your tenant peace of mind. Online rent payments are often tracked by credit agencies, which allows tenants to build their credit by paying their rent on time, something paying through more traditional methods doesn't do. And best of all, many online rent payment services let roommates split up the payment among them, so everyone automatically pays their share, even if those shares aren't equal (for instance, if the guy who gets stuck with the smallest bedroom gets to pay a smaller share of the rent). This avoids the classic roommate headache of one person forgetting to chip in each month.

The downside to electronic rent payment services is that they're pricey, at least when compared to the cost of a stamp. These services make their money by taking a small percentage from each payment. It's not a big amount, but landlords still need to compensate for it by either passing the expense along to the tenants by asking a higher rent, which could theoretically drive away some tenants, or by simply accepting that they'll make a little less each month. To me, the convenience of online rent payment services makes them more than worth the cost. Ever since I switched to online payments for my properties, I haven't looked back.

Consider whether you might require, or at least encourage, your tenants to obtain any specific forms of insurance. More and more landlords are requiring renter's insurance, particularly in the wake of natural disasters like Hurricane Sandy, which devastated numerous apartment buildings when it tore through New York and New Jersey.

In Europe, it's common for many tenants to seek out security deposit insurance as well, and now that's starting to become more

popular in the States. Personally, I'd love to see this trend continue, because the security deposit is one of the most common points of contention between landlords and tenants.

Every sitcom set in an apartment has made a joke about the security deposit at some point. ("Great, there goes my security deposit!" Cue laugh track.) But if you've ever rented an apartment, you know that security deposits are no laughing matter. They add a significant amount to the initial move-in costs, and an equally significant amount of stress when it's time to move out, as the tenants worry about whether or not they're going to get that money back.

A typical security deposit is equal to one month's rent. With security deposit insurance, instead of the tenant paying that to you, they pay a fraction of it—maybe 20 percent—as a one-time payment to the insurance company. That's major savings for the tenant off their move-in costs.

Now, unlike a normal security deposit, they're not going to get that money back, even if they take perfect care of the apartment. That initial deposit is nonrefundable. So why would they want to do it? Well, in addition to lowering their move-in costs, security deposit insurance can cover them for as much or even more than a month's rent. On a $1,600 apartment, an initial one-time payment of $320 might provide two thousand dollars' worth of coverage.

As a landlord, this is a great deal for you. Not only do you get more coverage than a normal security deposit, if there's any damage that needs fixing, you don't have to fight with your tenant about it. You just file a claim with their insurance company. When landlords and tenants fight about security deposits, it can get ugly fast. It's not uncommon for those disputes to end up in court, which takes time and can end up costing you more than the initial security deposit anyway. Security deposit insurance skips those headaches altogether. I highly recommend checking around to see if it's available in your area.

Always ask yourself, "What could I be doing to give my tenants a better experience?" Could the common areas be improved? Could the building be cleaner? Do you have spare space that could be put to use—maybe as a laundry room or play area? Is it time to touch up the paint to give the building that extra boost? When you run into a tenant in the hallway or outside the building, ask them, "How's the apartment working out for you? Anything we could be doing better?"

When you put energy and thought into your building, it encourages tenants to put energy and thought into how they maintain their apartments. But it can't just be all talk. You have to lead through action. For instance, you could offer your tenants a list of ways they can save energy and go green in their apartments, and a few tenants might pick up a pointer or two. But if you start swapping out the light fixtures in the common areas for ones with energy-saving bulbs, or replace your building's black tar roof with an environmentally friendly roof garden, it will send a strong and clear message to your tenants that you're serious about making the building greener, and they'll be more likely to pitch in.

Should You Use a Broker?

Given that becoming a broker and starting my own brokerage firm was the key to my path to success, you probably think I'm going to say yes and just be done with it. I certainly think that brokers offer a tremendously valuable service to both the tenants and the landlords they work with. But the truth is, deciding whether or not you should use a broker is a little more complicated than that. It depends on your circumstances and the nature of your local real estate market.

Different areas have different standard practices when it comes to working with brokers. In New York City, pretty much everyone gives their listings to a broker. Even giant management companies that keep people on their payroll whose only job is to advertise and show their vacant apartments still give their listings to brokers, just to ensure that those vacancies get filled as quickly as humanly

possible. The first person to bring in a qualified applicant, whether it's an internal employee or an outside broker, gets to keep the broker fee.

Out in the Bay Area, on the other hand, working with a broker is virtually unheard of for rentals. The most high-end properties might use a broker, but all the other management companies and private landlords just dump their open listings on Craigslist and wait for people to come to them. Demand out there is so ferocious that property managers hold open houses and will review multiple applications at once, just like a seller considering multiple bids.

And there are plenty of cities, such as LA, where landlords and management companies depend on brokers to advertise and fill their vacant apartments, but the tenant never pays the broker fee—it's always covered by the owner of the property. Any property manager who tried to pass the broker fee along to the tenant would be looked at as a crook.

Standards vary from market to market, and markets change over time. Even New York was not so reliant on brokers a few decades ago as it is now. And when I started Rapid Realty, no one was using brokers for rentals in the outer boroughs. That was just a Manhattan thing. Now it's everywhere.

The fact of the matter is, when you're first starting out as a property investor and you only have a few units to fill, you might be able to do it without the aid of a broker. In places where the property owner is the one who covers the broker fee, that's obviously the tempting route to take, because it means you hold onto more money. But you'd better be confident in your ability to advertise those units and get people to come check them out, because every month that those units stay empty is a month you're paying your building's mortgage and expenses out of your own savings.

So it depends on what sort of time you have available to be working on getting your vacancies filled. If you're dealing with few enough units that you can handle the responsibility of advertising and showing them every year, or however often they become available, then that's great. I know plenty of people who actually started out as landlords—some inherited rental properties from their families, others got into the property investment game after making some money in an unrelated field—who then decided to become real estate agents themselves because they found they actually enjoyed crafting ads and showing vacant apartments.

You might also be able to get by without the help of a broker if your vacant units are somehow unique; for instance, if they're priced well below market value, if they offer hotly sought-after features that most units in your area don't have (like a private yard in an urban area), or if they're located in an area where rental inventory is very scarce.

On the other hand, if you don't have the time to be showing your units all day, or your properties aren't located somewhere it would be easy for you to get to on a regular basis (many investors end up with properties scattered all over a city, or in multiple cities, or even multiple countries), or if your units don't stand out from the pack on their own, or you simply don't think you have the knack for advertising and showing prospective tenants, then working with a broker could be the smart bet right from the start.

In a place like New York where the tenant is often expected to pay the broker fee, what do you have to lose from working with a broker? It doesn't take a penny out of your pocket, and you get all the benefits of working with a team of professionals who do nothing all day other than promote vacant listings and match people with homes that fit their needs.

Anywhere else, it's a judgment call. Does the cost of a broker fee outweigh the cost of potentially having your units sit vacant? Most tenants are looking for a move-in date of the first or fifteenth of the month, which means that if those dates pass you by, and you don't have tenants lined up, you may need to wait until the next month to find someone. Is that a gamble you can afford to take? It's a call that every landlord has to make for themselves.

Keep It Professional

I've seen it a thousand times: a first-time, or aspiring first-time, property investor decides to buy a rental property and then immediately says, "I'll rent it to my friends! It'll be great!"

No. No, it won't.

This is a prime example of a situation where your heart and your gut may come into conflict. But the single most important piece of advice I can give if you're new to property investment is this: Don't rent to your friends. At least, not at first.

Every landlord-to-be thinks that renting their units to their friends is the best possible situation. And why wouldn't you? After all, it means you'd already know and have a great relationship with your tenants, which feels awesome, especially if you've never managed a rental property before. And you can trust your friends to pay their rent, because they would never want to make things awkward between you. Hell, if you gave them a little break on the rent, they'd probably even pitch in around the building!

It's doubly tempting because you probably have some friends who could really use a cool landlord like you. If you live in a big city, even if you've never had a bad rental experience yourself, you almost certainly have a friend who has: the one who has to move every six months because they can't find someone willing to give them a longer lease, the one who keeps finding great apartments and then getting kicked out because the owner decides to turn them into condos, the one who just got screwed by a giant rent increase that skirts the limit of legality. You could help them all. You'd be a hero!

Resist. As tempting as it is to give in to those noble impulses, resist. Because if you take a little time and really think about it, you'll find that, as great as it all sounds, something about it doesn't sit easy with you. That's your gut talking, and it has a good point.

First of all, that discount on the rent you were thinking of offering—can you really afford it? I'm not asking if you *think* you can afford it, I'm asking if you've actually taken the time to crunch the numbers, because every dollar you lower the rent is increasing the time it will take you to make your full return on investment. Especially if this is your first building, you need to be very careful about being able to cover your mortgage, taxes, utilities, maintenance fees, and still leave yourself enough to cover any sudden, unforeseen repairs.

So, after all that, are you sure you can afford to offer that discount? You are? Terrific! Now, next question—can you afford to not get paid at all?

Right now, you might be thinking, *Anthony, you don't know what you're talking about. My friend would never stiff me on the rent!*

I'm 100 percent sure you're right. Your friend would never *mean* to stiff you. They would have every intention of paying on time every month, of being a model tenant, and of gratefully enjoying the apartment you're renting to them without ever being a pain in your side.

But then comes the month when they're a little late on the rent—past the grace period you set in the lease (you *did* make them sign a lease, right?). You don't say anything, or maybe you shoot them a quick, nonjudgmental reminder. Hey, everyone makes mistakes, right? Not a big deal. They pay up, and they're embarrassed that it ever got so late in the month.

Then a few months later, they ask if they can get a little extension on the rent. Money's a little tight this month. They're stretched pretty thin. Can you give them a break? You know what it's like to look at your bank account and be worried by what you see. And it's your friend, for crying out loud. They wouldn't be asking if they didn't really need it. So you tell them it's no problem. Maybe you even cut them a deal on that month's rent.

Then a little while after that, they're late again, and you don't want to say anything, because it was awkward enough the first time, and hey, maybe they're still having some financial trouble. So you let it go, and you let it go, and it slips off your radar when something else in your life pops up, and before you know it, you've just gone the full month without receiving your rent check.

No one in this scenario set out to screw over anyone else. No one was necessarily acting in bad faith. Maybe your friend really did just forget! But you still ended up getting the short end of the stick, and your friend still ended up taking advantage of you. And it happened because you, understandably, wanted to preserve your friendship. You didn't want to be the kind of friend who lets money come between you. You wanted to be a good guy.

This is not a fantasy scenario. This is something that happens to new landlords every single day.

It may not always be in the form of skipping rent payments. It can happen in other ways. But one way or another, it's all too common for friends to take advantage of their friends when they enter into a tenant-landlord situation. The landlord thinks their friend will take better care of their property than the average tenant, but actually the opposite is true—because of your personal relationship, your friend is actually *less* likely to take consistently good care of your property, because deep down they know you'll cut them some slack.

What inevitably happens is that you end up losing money compared to a tenant with whom you have only a professional relationship, and even worse, you can often end up losing the friend. Once someone takes advantage of you like that, even if they weren't doing it consciously or maliciously, once resentment over money enters the relationship, it's hard to come back from that.

So, for the sake of your budget, your future, and your friendships, don't rent to your friends. At least, not until you've spent a few years getting comfortable enough with maintaining landlord-tenant relationships and collecting rent in a timely fashion that you can separate your professional relationship with your personal relationship without risking them both.

PART 7

The Art of Negotiation

Some General Observations

The real estate business involves a lot of negotiation. So do most other businesses, for that matter. You want something from another person; that other person wants something from you—you discuss, you bargain—and with good will on both sides, you'll work it out. Many people regard negotiation as a contest, in which your objective is to get whatever you want without regard to what the other person wants. If you take that approach, you'll seldom win—and in the long run, nobody will want to deal with you. A negotiation can have winners and losers, but regarding negotiation as a zero-sum game is the road to ruin.

A zero-sum game is one where there's a certain prize to be won, or a set sum to be divided. There's a winner and a loser: one side gets the prize and the other doesn't. Or one side gets more of the amount to be divided, and the other gets less. Almost never can you split the herring exactly down the backbone.

In many cases, it's possible to avoid the zero-sum mindset and create a situation where both sides walk away at least partly satisfied. The ideal outcome, some people say, is when both sides feel that the other side has been equally inconvenienced, and each side feels that it has won a little more than the other side has. This "win-win" outcome is possible if you can get past the idea that both sides are competing for the same prize. Usually, you can do this by creating value for both sides.

Both sides should feel that they've won at least some of their objectives.

If Person A feels that Person B has unfairly outnegotiated him, he'll refuse to cooperate with B in the future. Furthermore, word will get around that B is a trickster. Therefore, whomever you're negotiating with—a superior, a subordinate, a peer, an outsider—you should strive to get a good deal for everyone.

This will require a degree of trust, because you have to regard the win-win process as collaborative rather than adversarial. In an adversarial situation, you can't let the other side know much about what you want, what you have to have, what your deadline is, or any other information that they might use to your detriment. In a collaborative situation, you have to trust the other side with as much information as you can give them, so that they can help you to achieve what you want, in the time frame that's available to you.

You need to know what your alternatives are.

No matter whom you're negotiating with, you need to be able to walk away and deal with someone else if negotiations break down. Otherwise, you're begging, not bargaining.

Never present an ultimatum ("If I don't get a 20 percent raise, then I'll quit!") unless you're prepared to carry out the "then" part. An ultimatum is by its nature nonnegotiable. If the answer's no, then you have a choice of quitting then and there (and do you have a new job lined up?) or backing down and looking like a fool.

By the same token, don't accept an ultimatum from the other party, or take his word that something is nonnegotiable. Instead, say something like, "Let's work together to find a solution that I can afford, that won't make you decide to quit," or, "Since you say this item is nonnegotiable, let's find a solution that will let me get along without it."

Be generous when your adversary is reasonable.

If he asks for something that you consider fair, and that you can easily give, give it without quibbling. But that's a good time for you to bring up requests that he, in turn, can easily grant!

Do your homework.

If one of the issues is simply money—for example, if you're negotiating the price of a property, or your salary—come into the negotiations well-researched. Get as much information as you can about the prices of similar properties in that neighborhood, or about what other companies are paying employees whose functions are similar to yours. Don't be afraid to ask for a little more, or offer a little less—but be realistic in your expectations.

The other side won't always tell you what their weaknesses are, but you can try to figure them out. Maybe, for instance, they need to get a property sold by the end of their fiscal year, for tax purposes. Or maybe they need to raise capital in a hurry to avoid a foreclosure. Maybe they're depending on a big order from you to avoid laying off employees. A zero-sum negotiator will use this information to take advantage, to play hardball. A win-win negotiator will know this weakness and will exploit it if he has to, but will first take the approach of trying to help the other side solve that problem.

Don't speak first.

It's a commonly held belief that the person who speaks first in a negotiation is usually the one who loses. The reason behind this is simple math.

Every time you make an offer in a negotiation, you're narrowing your own possibilities. If you offer a tenant $15,000 to buy them out of their apartment so you can renovate, for instance, you generally can't offer $12,000 a minute later. Likewise, a seller who says they're willing to take $500,000 for a house can't suddenly

turn around and tell you they want $600,000. (The exception to this, of course, is when there's a bidding war, which can drive the sale price of a home well above its asking price. But that's not a true negotiation, since all the parties involved typically don't get to know what the others are offering.)

The first person to make an offer in a negotiation, whether it's to say what they're willing to give or what they're willing to take, has just set their own ceiling for the best they can possibly do in this deal. If a tenant tells you, "I'll move out for $8,000" right out of the gate, they might never know that your opening offer was going to be $10,000.

Negotiating very rarely ends with either party getting their initial offer. That's why good negotiators start by asking for more than they realistically expect. But the person who makes the first move is still most likely to be the one who ends up taking the biggest step down from where they began.

Know and address your weaknesses.

If you have weaknesses, see if you can cure them before the negotiation process begins. If you really want to buy a certain property, find one or two others that are almost as good—properties that you could be happy enough with if you had to settle for one of them. If you're negotiating for a big order that you're not sure you're going to get, start thinking of how you'll keep your business going without it. Always let the other side know that you're considering these other options.

Never take negotiations personally.

But do keep personalities in mind. The other guy isn't driving a hard bargain because he dislikes you, but because this is business and he wants a good deal just as much as you do. Stay as polite and cordial as you can be during the process; be courteous and considerate. Your attitude will go a long way toward working out a deal.

If, on the other hand, you sense that the person you're negotiating with is a liar, a bully, a manipulator—well, that is why you must always be willing to walk away.

Never denigrate the other side's position. That is to say, don't tell him he's lucky that you're making him such a good offer for such a lousy property. Don't tell him you know of another factory that could fill your order faster and cheaper. Don't ever imply that there's anything wrong or second-rate about what he's offering.

Keep your goal in mind.

Your goal is not to get the better of the other guy. Your objective is to buy or sell the property, or get hired to fill an order, or to settle a conflict. If you can convince the other party that you want both sides to walk away happy, you'll have a foundation of trust—and then the two of you can work together on solving the problem.

Ask for more than you expect to get.

Make three lists for yourself. The first list is "things I have to get as part of this deal." The second is "things I want, but could do without if I had to." The third is "things that don't really matter, but I wouldn't mind having." But don't tell the other side which of those items are on which list. Just ask for all of them. You never know: the other side might not give you any pushback at all about your must-haves. They might only object to a few small points that you don't really care about. In that case, you can say, "Fine," and shake hands.

Whatever deal you arrive at, get it in writing and signed by both parties. As the old saying goes, "An oral contract ain't worth the paper it's printed on."

PART 8

The Art of the Buyout

When you buy a multiunit building, your goal is to increase its profitability. After all, if the building were already maximizing its earning potential, why would the previous owner have wanted to sell it? Boosting profitability means increasing the rent roll, which means raising rents, usually through renovating the units so they command a higher price.

In a perfect world, any building you buy would come in one of two states:

1. Totally unoccupied, allowing you to come in and renovate any way you like so you can ask for a higher rent, or
2. Fully occupied with tenants who have no problem with you coming in and raising their rents (presumably they can just pay for the increase with the profits from their unicorn farms, since this is clearly a fantasy scenario).

Ninety-nine percent of the time, any building you buy is going to come partially or completely occupied. But you can't get in there to renovate if the current tenants don't want to leave. With your profits hanging by a thread, even a single tenant refusing to move can turn a great deal into a nightmare. That's why you need to understand the art of the buyout: knowing what to offer tenants—and just as importantly, how to offer it—to make them comfortable with moving out, without costing you so much that you can kiss any whiff of profits from this investment goodbye. If you don't have the finesse and savvy to do it right, you can see your entire investment go up in smoke.

For many investors, tenant buyouts may be your first brush with the dark side of real estate. No one *likes* asking people to leave their homes. And pop culture is loaded with the image of the greedy landlord coming in and forcing tenants (often sweet old ladies) out onto the street. But real estate is a business, and you have a right to seek a return on your investment. Just remember: you might have to buy out some tenants, but that doesn't mean you have to be the bad guy.

I've negotiated hundreds of tenant buyouts over the years, both for my own investment properties and as a hired consultant for other landlords who were unsure how to handle these delicate situations on their own. I've even been hired to negotiate on behalf of tenants who worried they weren't going to get a fair shake. After all those negotiations, there's one thing I can say for sure: no two tenant buyouts are exactly alike, because no two tenants are exactly alike. Everyone's situation is unique to them. But here are a few tips you should keep in mind before walking into any buyout scenario:

Know the law: Rent control and rent stabilization laws prevent tenants from having landlords come in and kick them out or jack up their rent. In this case, the landlord is you. Every city and state's rent control/stabilization laws are different. Make sure you know your local laws and ordinances *before* you buy. You don't want to learn what it feels like to realize you're stuck with a bad investment and see your profits go up in smoke. Take your time and do your homework first.

Buyout is a dirty word: Want to know the fastest way to turn a tenant against you in a negotiation? Tell them it's a buyout. Even though that's exactly what it is—you are literally there to buy them out of their apartment—and even though you may have every intention of being fair and even generous, the word *buyout* makes people think of some sneering, moustache-twirling villain

coming to kick little old ladies out into the cold, or some greedy, cigar-chomping Wall Street fatcat crushing some poor mom-and-pop business under his heel. You pick which one's worse. So, by all means, be upfront and honest with the tenants when you speak to them; just leave *buyout* out of your vocabulary.

Put yourself in their shoes: Imagine that you've been living in an apartment for just a few months and you find out that the building has been sold, and now the new owner is planning on clearing out the building so he can renovate. Sure, it's inconvenient. But maybe you don't have a whole lot of attachment to the building, so the windfall of a possible buyout appeals to you. Maybe you already have another housing option open to you. It's no big deal. You may even come out ahead!

But what if you really liked that apartment? What if you moved into that building because it's right where you needed to be for work, or school, or your kid's school, or to be near an ailing family member? What if your credit isn't great and you had a hell of a time finding an apartment the last time around, especially one that would let you keep your dog, and you can't imagine having to start looking again?

What if you hadn't been living in that apartment for just a few months, but thirty years? There's no two ways about it: it would feel like someone was coming to take away your home.

Talk to the previous owner about the tenants in the building before you finalize the purchase. Ask how long they've been there, ask what they're like, find out anything and everything you can about their situation, so you have a better idea of what sort of negotiations and considerations you've got in front of you. Every tenant is unique, and some will need more care than others. Thinking about the situation from their perspective will make it easier for you to identify what they would need to accept the buyout.

Here are just a few of my most memorable tenant buyout experiences:

I Get into the Game

There's no teacher like experience.

My first experience with tenant buyouts came when I least expected it.

A certain landlord had been working with me for years, counting on me to rent out the other five units in her six-family building. Every time I went over to her building, I'd leave my card on her refrigerator. One day I got a call at seven in the morning from a young lady who said she was the landlord's niece.

"My aunt is ill," she explained. "We're up from Florida to take her home with us. She's always said good things about you. She's given us control of her property, but we want nothing to do with it. Can you sell it? I don't care how much you get for it, as long as you sell it within a week so we don't have to keep traveling back and forth."

One week to sell a six-family building? It was a tall order, but there was a simple, yet elegant solution: I bought it myself! Because of my great relationship with the owner, the niece sold it to me for a song: just $150,000.

I knew the building was rent-stabilized, and I knew that meant I was very limited in how much I could adjust the current tenants' rent. I assumed I could just wait until the tenants' leases expired, then simply choose not to renew them. That way, the tenants would move out and I could renovate the whole place. But you know what they say about what happens when you assume…

What I didn't know at the time was that the rent stabilization laws said I had to renew the tenants' leases whether I wanted to or not. They could renew their leases as many times as they wanted, and there wasn't a thing I could do about it.

I'd just jumped into the deep end of real estate investment without realizing it. Now I had no choice but to individually negotiate a buyout of every tenant in the building. So that's precisely what I did. And by the time I was done, and I could finally get in and renovate the building like I wanted, well...let's just say I'd spent a lot more than my initial $150,000 investment.

Those first experiences taught me volumes about the risks and rewards of buying investment properties, lessons I still carry with me. I still own the building, which today is worth more than $3.5 million!

Lolli's Lesson: Always do your homework. Because I foolishly assumed that I understood rent stabilization laws without actually checking to make sure that I was right, I ended up taking on a lot more work and expense than I originally anticipated. In this case, it still ended up being a smart investment, but if a single tenant had flat-out refused to accept a buyout, it would have been a disaster.

The Park Slope Roomies

When tenants ask for the impossible, sometimes the best thing you can do is give it to them.

A pair of roommates in a building I'd just purchased made it clear they had no intention of moving out. They were living in a railroad-style two-bedroom that was falling apart around their ears, but they wouldn't budge. Why? Simple: They were only paying $800 a month between the two of them, and their lease was rent-stabilized. In other words, they'd found a unicorn, and they weren't about to give it up because they didn't like the shape of its horn.

After talking it over, the roommates told me that the only way they would move was if I found them a two-bedroom in Park Slope, one of the most desirable—and expensive—neighborhoods in Brooklyn, with central air, something they didn't have in their current apartment. And they wouldn't pay more than $1,000 a month.

It was an impossible task, and I knew it. They might as well have asked for a solid gold Jacuzzi and a robot butler. But then I happened to get a call from a client I'd worked with many times before, an actor who frequently appeared on HBO. His work often kept him out of town for months at a time, and I'd helped him find short-term tenants to rent his condo: a two-bedroom with central air in Park Slope. This time around, the actor wanted me to rent out his place on a long-term basis. He was looking for $1,700 a month, which was on the high end of the spectrum at the time, but certainly not unheard of. I asked if he'd take $1,000 a month instead. The actor just laughed.

Two days later, though, the actor called me again and asked me if I knew any good mortgage brokers who could help him refinance. He confessed that he hadn't landed any gigs in a while and he was now six months behind on his mortgage payments, to the tune of $6,000.

I made him an offer: rent the condo to the two roommates for $1,000 a month and they'll pay their first six months up front. Seeing a shining opportunity to get out of debt and keep his condo, the actor agreed. I paid for the roommates' first six months out of my own pocket, and just like that, the roommates were able to move out of their crumbling railroad apartment into a beautiful Park Slope condo with separate bedrooms and central air, where they lived rent-free for six months. And I was able to renovate their apartment and make good on my plans for the building.

Lolli's Lesson: Okay, I'm not going to lie, there was a pretty fair amount of luck on my side on this one. But it just goes to show, sometimes you have to think outside the box. If I had just scoured the market to find a $1,000 two-bedroom apartment in Park Slope with central air, I'd probably still be looking today. But by utilizing my connections and introducing new parties and new circumstances into the negotiation—something that always comes with its own risks—I ended up saving my investment.

The Asian Persuasion

Negotiating a buyout is complicated enough, but what do you do when the tenant doesn't even speak your language?

I'd just purchased a building in prime Park Slope and wanted to give it a thorough renovation. This was a concept I had a hard time communicating to the tenant on the first floor: an old Asian woman who didn't speak a word of English. I tried talking to her through her nurse, only to discover that she didn't speak English either! How could I explain to the woman that I wanted to renovate her apartment when I couldn't even tell her who I was?

I went on Craigslist and posted an ad offering fifty dollars to anyone who could help me translate a single message into Mandarin: "Do you have any family who speaks English? I'm your new landlord, and I need to make some repairs."

Hoping that the translator had done a good job, I hand-delivered the translated message to the old woman. She read it over, then added a note of her own in Chinese characters. I had to go back to the translator to find out what she had said. For all I knew, the old woman had just told me to go to hell.

Fortunately, it turned out to be nothing so rude. What she had written was the name and contact info of her grandson, who owned a house on Staten Island. Perfect! Not only had I found a mediator for the negotiation, but maybe this guy would even be willing to take her in, which would save me the trouble of finding her a new apartment.

I got in touch with him, but it didn't go as well as I'd hoped. The man told me he hadn't spoken to his grandmother in ten years, and he had no interest whatsoever in having her come to stay with him.

I'd already bought the building. There was no going back now, but the purchase had depended on my being able to renovate all the units. The old woman's apartment was rent-controlled and she was paying only $250 a month—a tiny fraction of what the apartment could be worth. If I couldn't renovate her unit, the whole deal would be a bust!

So, I offered the grandson $25,000 to convert the basement of his house in Staten Island into an apartment for his grandmother, plus $1,000 a month to cover her rent for the next two years. Soon there was a terrific new apartment waiting for the old woman, and she was even reunited with family she hadn't seen in a decade. I was able to renovate the entire building, as I had hoped. Years later, the building went condo and I converted the first-floor unit into a two-bedroom duplex with a private garden—and sold it for $900,000. Not bad, for a total cost to me of $49,000.

Lolli's Lesson: There are a couple of takeaways here: You have to be ready to think outside the box. If I hadn't gone on Craigslist to translate a message, or I hadn't tried to see if the grandson would take in his grandmother, or I hadn't paid to create an apartment for her where none existed before, the whole deal would have fallen through.

Perhaps more importantly, you need to be prepared to deal with people whose backgrounds and experiences are totally foreign to you. It helps if you speak another language—I was fortunate to grow up speaking both English and Spanish—but sooner or later you're bound to encounter someone whose language is different from yours, or whose customs are alien to you. It's important to be sensitive to those differences and remember that, as much as it may feel like this person represents an obstacle that has come into your life, you are also an unusual circumstance that has come into theirs.

The Trumpet Player

When tenants have unusual needs, sometimes you need to go the extra mile.

A tenant was willing to move out, and he even said he'd pay up to $1,100 for a new place (up from the $800 he'd been paying). It just had to be near Prospect Park. And one other tiny little thing: the tenant was a jazz trumpet player who needed to be able to play anytime he felt inspired, even in the dead of night!

I showed him one place after another, all of them near the park and within his budget. Each time, the musician insisted—quite considerately—on meeting the landlord and all of the neighbors so he could ask them if they would be okay with him playing his trumpet at three in the morning. Unsurprisingly, the responses ranged from "Please don't" to "No way!"

Another apartment I thought the musician might like was farther away from the park. Convincing him to go see it was like trying to throw a cat out the window. At last, the musician finally agreed to take a look. Sure enough, he loved it! It might not have been right by the park, but it made up for it in space. And unlike where the musician had been living, this place was in beautiful shape, as it had just been renovated. In fact, the neighboring apartment was being renovated right then.

The musician spoke to the man overseeing the renovations, who turned out to be the landlord. As he'd done before, the musician asked him if he'd be okay with him playing his trumpet at five in the morning. The landlord's eyes went wide.

"I knew I recognized you!" he said. "I've seen you play at the Blue Note a dozen times! You're amazing! You can play anytime you want!"

Needless to say, the musician took the apartment. He was so grateful for the help, he even invited me to come hear him play! Total cost of buyout: $0.00

Lolli's Lesson: This was another lucky break, for sure. But this was also an ideal outcome that wouldn't have happened if I hadn't convinced the trumpet player to go see an apartment farther from the park. And he wouldn't have gone to see the apartment farther from the park if I hadn't first showed him a whole array of apartments near the park that ended up not being a good fit for him. Even if I somehow had known that there was a landlord out there who loved his music and would be thrilled to have him in his building, there's no way I could have talked him into going to see that apartment without showing him the places by the park first. Perseverance goes a long way in this business. This is an important lesson whether you're a landlord or a broker: sometimes, even when you know you're right, there's no better way to convince someone than to let them see it for themselves.

With Friends like These

When a tenant brings in a friend to negotiate on their behalf, sometimes the best thing to do is bring the friend in on the deal.

One tenant refused to speak to me at all. I was prepared to make her a very reasonable and straightforward offer, but she wouldn't hear it. Instead, she insisted that any and all negotiations go through her best friend, a no-nonsense woman who worked as a corrections officer.

From the moment that I met the officer, she came at me in full-on, hardcore, I-eat-punks-like-you-for-breakfast-and-then-I-go-break-up-a-prison-riot mode. She got up in my face, shouting that her friend wouldn't move for a penny less than $75,000, and that was that.

I told her the offer was $10,000. That didn't go over well. The officer told me in no uncertain terms what I could do with my offer. It was $75,000 or nothing.

I asked her, "If I give you $5,000, would you convince your friend to move for $10,000?"

Her response? "Okay!"

Lolli's Lesson: It's not uncommon in any negotiation for one party to bring in a representative—a friend, a relative, even a professional like me—who they think is a tougher negotiator and will be able to get a better deal than they would be able to get on their own. This representative will usually come in treating you like the enemy. But if you can turn them from an enemy into a friend, you're golden.

This story is also the perfect example of why you should never open any negotiation with the maximum amount you're able to pay. This buyout ended up costing me $15,000, 50 percent more than my initial offer, but that didn't break my budget or put me in a position where I couldn't afford to renovate my investment property, because I left myself some room to maneuver.

The Bigger They Are...

There are three kinds of tenants: ones that are receptive to a buyout, ones that are resistant to a buyout, and ones who try to kill you!

A landlord had hired me to negotiate a buyout on his behalf with a tenant who was completely refusing to move. I gave the tenant a call and we struck up a conversation. Everything seemed to be going fine, until the guy suddenly snapped. It was like someone had flipped a switch. One moment we were having a perfectly civil discussion, the next the tenant was screaming, "I know who you are, I know where you work, and I'm going to come down to your office and kick your ass!" I heard the tenant slam the phone down like it had just bitten his ear, and the line went dead.

Five minutes later, the tenant showed up outside my office, shouting and ranting at the top of his lungs. The guy was huge— six foot eight, built like a defensive tackle, and clearly furious. I went outside to try to calm him down.

As soon as he saw me, the man roared, "I run this hood! This is my block! I'm not going nowhere!"

Before I could even get a word in, the man pulled out a knife and lunged at me! I jumped back in the nick of time: the blade missed cutting my insides out by about an inch. The man advanced on me, ready to attack again—but he stopped in his tracks when he noticed that we weren't alone. My entire staff had come outside and had witnessed the whole thing. He may have also noticed the video cameras outside the office, which had recorded every second.

The police arrested the man and searched his apartment, where they found drug paraphernalia, weapons, and his young child, who had been left there alone. They also found the phone lying off the hook from when the man had slammed it down on the receiver.

A lot of people might have washed their hands of the whole deal after that, but as far as I was concerned, the attempted stabbing had put me in a pretty strong negotiating position. I offered the tenant a deal: I wouldn't press charges if he just moved out. The tenant wisely agreed. Total cost of buyout: not even the price of a new pair of underpants, thank goodness.

Lolli's Lesson: There's something to be said here about leverage and negotiating from a position of strength, but the real lesson is this: real estate is about people's homes, and people take anything concerning their homes personally. This particular guy was clearly not in his right mind—to this day, I still have no idea what I said that set him off so suddenly and violently—but even in less extreme circumstances, people can get volatile. You will get screamed at, that's unavoidable. But, hey, hopefully you won't get stabbed.

The New Homeowner

> When a tenant has a difficult situation that makes it almost impossible for them to move, don't just change your offer: change their life.

A man living in a rent-stabilized apartment in a building I'd just purchased turned out to be in a tough situation. He was unemployed and living on disability, which meant he couldn't afford to pay for a more expensive apartment even if he wanted to—nor could he risk moving someplace where the rent could suddenly spike. I made him a generous offer, but the man crunched the numbers and figured that even if a new apartment didn't suddenly raise the rent on him, the money would still last only three years. The only way he would move, he said, was if I found him another rent-stabilized apartment, a nearly impossible feat.

Instead, I convinced the man to take the money I was offering him and use it as the down payment on his very own condo. It would enable him to get a beautiful new place to live, and since mortgage payments are not subject to annual increases like rent, he would never have to worry about his monthly payment suddenly rising beyond what he could manage on his fixed income.

The tenant was stunned. Living on disability, he had never dreamed that he might one day own his own home. He agreed to the deal, and I personally found him a great studio condo that fit his budget. I was able to renovate my apartment, and the man who had been living with the constant fear of being unable to pay his rent was now a proud homeowner!

Lolli's Lesson: When you go into a tenant buyout, your mindset should not be, *how much do I have to pay to get this person to move?* It should be, *what's stopping this person from moving, and what can I do about it?* Most of the time—yes—the answer is money. But sometimes there's something you can actually fix for somebody, and that adds a tremendous amount of value to any offer.

You Can't Win 'Em All

Being a savvy investor means knowing when to walk away.

I got a call from the owner of a building in Park Slope. I was intrigued; the building was in a spectacular location and it had a lot of potential. The only issue was that the three-bedroom apartment on the top floor was rent-controlled, and the tenant had been there for ages and wasn't likely to want to leave. The owner told me that the tenant was a single old man, eighty-two and feeble, and suggested that I just buy the building and, well, wait for the inevitable.

I insisted on meeting the gentleman himself before making any decisions. It was a walkup building, and as I climbed the stairs, I heard salsa music playing. By the time I got to the top, the music was so loud that I had to pound on the door with all my might just to be heard. The door opened, and I was shocked to see the so-called feeble old man nimbly dancing along to the lively music. He wasn't half bad, either!

It was clear that the old man was in excellent health for his age, but there were still a lot of stairs between his apartment and the front door. I offered to set him up with a two-bedroom apartment on a lower floor in the building in exchange for the three-bedroom where he was living by himself.

The old man took me into the master bedroom. "See this bed?" he asked. "My wife died right there, and I'm going to die right here."

I just smiled and thanked the man for his time. As I walked down the stairs to leave, I looked back up and saw the old man single-handedly carrying a large metal laundry cart down the stairs behind him. This guy wasn't going anywhere anytime soon.

I shook the owner's hand and thanked him for thinking of me. I'd negotiated with some tough customers in the past, but as nice as the building was, it wasn't worth going toe-to-toe with the old man on the top floor.

Lolli's Lesson: If a deal seems like a great opportunity except for one detail, it's not a great opportunity. Don't get caught up in visions of what things might be like if that one detail weren't in your way. Invest based on what the reality is, not what you want the reality to be.

My Way or the Highway

What do you do when a great opportunity comes at the worst possible time?

Two men walked into my office one day. They said they had two buildings nearby that they wanted to sell. I was interested, but I'd just bought another building around the corner and was waiting to recover my liquidity before I acquired any more properties. Still, these were great buildings, and I hated the idea of missing out on the opportunity.

I told the men I'd buy their buildings, but only if they agreed to my terms: I would buy out the current tenants and renovate the buildings all at my own expense, then I'd rerent the apartments at a higher rate. While I did this, I'd pay the men the equivalent of the rent they were currently collecting each month. If they agreed to let me do that for six months, I was certain I'd have the liquidity to close on the deal, and the higher rent roll would allow me to get a better rate on the mortgages. If they didn't take this deal, I'd have to pass.

It was an unusual offer, to be sure: a far cry from what the owners had been hoping for. If I couldn't get the current tenants to move out, or the renovations took longer than expected, or I couldn't find new tenants to pay the higher rent, the whole deal would fall apart. It was a big risk. But they'd come to Anthony Lolli for a reason.

The two men agreed, and I got to work. I bought out every tenant, renovated both buildings, and swiftly filled every unit at the new, higher rate. Each month, I paid the men the equivalent of their old rent roll, and after six months, just as I'd promised, I bought both buildings with the money I'd made off the higher rents.

Lolli's Lesson: Reputation is key in this business. If I hadn't developed a reputation as an investor who is always as good as his word, there's no way these guys would have agreed to such an unusual deal. In fact, there's no way they would have approached me about buying their buildings in the first place. You can't develop a good reputation overnight; you have to earn it. But once you do, it always pays dividends.

The Real Estate School

Sometimes it's not the offer that counts; it's the person who makes it.

In 2004, I gave my parents their own real estate school, located on the floor above Rapid Realty's flagship office. Within a few years, both Rapid and the school were ready to expand. It made sense for Rapid to take over the upper floor, so I went looking for a building nearby that could serve as a bigger and better home for the school.

I found a suitable space just around the block and the very next day I got a certified check for $75,000 to use as a down payment. I was on my way to give the check to the seller's attorney when I noticed that a FOR SALE sign had just appeared on another building across the street.

I went over to take a closer look. By luck, the owner was there. He was an older man with a sickly yellow tinge to his eyes. He told me he was dying of kidney failure and his two children were arguing over what to do with the property. He wanted to sell it and split the money between them so he could put a stop to the fighting before he died.

The owner also happened to mention that he owned the building next door, although he quickly added that it wasn't for sale. I asked if I could see it anyway, and the owner reluctantly agreed. The moment I laid eyes on it, I could tell that it was a perfect space for the school, even better than the one I'd been about to buy. I told the owner how I felt, but the man flatly refused. It was not for sale; that was final.

Throughout our conversation, I'd been noticing that this old man spoke with an Ecuadorian accent. I quickly called my mother, who's an Ecuadorian immigrant, and who was the administrator of the school at the time. She was the perfect person to present my case. She was there within ten minutes. As she started talking to the old guy in Ecuadorian Spanish, his face lit up—and I knew we had a deal. I bought the mixed-use building for $900,000.

Lolli's Lesson: OK, this one is not technically a tenant buyout story, but it illustrates an important point: when a negotiation is stalling out, sometimes the best tactic is to find common ground. And often it doesn't matter if that common ground is even tied to the subject of the negotiation.

In this case, our shared heritage turned out to be the key to gaining this seller's favor. But I've also had situations where the guy across the negotiation table was wearing a Mets cap, and we got to talking about baseball for a while. I've even had negotiations that were going nowhere suddenly turn in my favor because I complimented my opponent's watch. After all, if there's one thing you should know about me by now, it's that I've always appreciated a good watch. Just finding that little patch of common ground is enough to redefine the relationship between you and your fellow negotiator and turn a bad deal into the deal of a lifetime.

CONCLUSION
Lolli's Top 10 Takeaways

1. Real estate matters. Real estate fulfills a basic human need for shelter and security. Any real estate transaction—whether it's a rental or a sale—is one of the largest and most important decisions of a person's life. Understanding that is the key to becoming the kind of real estate professional that people want to work with again and again.

2. The best sort of business you can get is a referral. People have a preconceived notion that anyone who works in real estate is sleazy and solely self-interested. With each new client, you have to work to dispel that notion. But a referral client comes in already predisposed to like you, because you came recommended by a friend who vouched for your services. You're already a big step closer to earning that client's trust. You can't buy that sort of client relationship; you have to earn it one client at a time.

3. There is absolutely no substitute for hard work. Don't believe anyone who tells you otherwise. You can't complain about the results you don't get in life from the work you didn't put in. The fact is, if you only kinda, sorta hustle, you'll only kinda, sorta succeed. Develop good work habits early on, and they'll serve you well your whole career. You have to go hard until hard isn't hard anymore.

4. If you're not setting yourself up to succeed, you're setting yourself up to fail. Preparation and education are the unshakable

foundations of success. If you're going to get into an industry, you have to learn everything you can about it. Otherwise, you're just asking to make the same mistakes and stumble into the same pitfalls that other failed businesses have fallen into before.

5. Visualize and focus. Set clear goals for yourself and visualize what you're working toward. Having a clear picture in your mind of what you're working toward will give you a constant source of motivation to draw from, and will keep you going forward in your toughest times. If you want to live like others can't, you'll need the motivation to work like others won't.

6. You already have your two best advisors—your heart and your gut. Your heart will tell you when something is the right thing to do. Your gut will tell you when something's going wrong, and you need to make a change. If they're ever telling you two conflicting things, trust your gut. It will be better in the long run, even if it doesn't feel that way at the time. Follow your heart to make yourself feel good, trust your gut to prevent yourself from feeling worse.

7. Negativity is the enemy of productivity. Put some distance between yourself and any doubtcasters in your life, whether they're coworkers who just want someone to complain to or friends or family members who claim to mean well but are more interested in saying "I told you so" than being supportive. This is especially true when you're first starting out in a business like real estate, which requires total commitment.

8. Know your strengths—and your weaknesses. You'll have to blow through a lot of barriers on your road to success, and you'll constantly redefine your own limits every step of the way, but one thing you won't be able to change is that you're only human. As your organization grows, you will reach a point where you can't do it all. Giving up control, either by expanding your team and delegating responsibility or by taking on a partner, can be one of the hardest things for an entrepreneur to do, but it is a necessary step on the timeline of every successful venture.

9. Don't follow the crowd when you can lead the pack. When it comes to investing, don't waste your time trying to find a deal where everyone else is already looking. If one market is getting crowded, it means you've already missed the best opportunities. Instead, try to anticipate where the crowd is going to go next so you can get in on the ground floor.

10. Master the art of negotiation. Every entrepreneur needs to be a skilled negotiator, and that goes double for anyone who wants to buy and sell real estate for a living. Remember to put yourself in the other person's shoes, and be ready to think outside the box. A creative solution can often save you from an expensive one.

As an entrepreneur armed with these tips, the only limits to what you can accomplish are your imagination and your drive. There will be obstacles in your way, but they will just make your accomplishments that much sweeter. The road to the top is never easy, but the view from the top is worth every ounce of effort.

I'll see you there.

Acknowledgments

I've always read these acknowledgment pages in books and thought to myself: where would I begin if I ever had to write one? Well, the day finally arrived, and as I sit here writing this, I—like many others in my position—am trying to remember the names of all the people who have had an influence on my life and had a hand in getting me where I am today. Since this is my first book and it includes an abbreviated version of my life story, to me it's important to thank the people who played a role in shaping me as an individual and helping me along the way.

I want to start by thanking my family, who have always played a critical role in my career, as you'll see in the first section of this book. My father **Nicholas Lolli** was a great man who taught me many life lessons and was a great influence on my decision to go the entrepreneurial route. He also taught me to win with integrity and not to burn bridges along the way. I'm grateful for having him in my life for as long as I did before he passed.

My mother **Gladys** is also an inspiration to me and has been by my side, serving as an advisor to me, in every major business and personal decision I've ever made. To this day I respect my mother's wise counsel and ask her to weigh in with her opinion. I love them both and will forever be grateful for their efforts in raising me to be the man I am today.

My parents taught me to make wise decisions in both my business and my personal life. I believe that one of the wisest decisions I made was choosing **Tereza** to spend the rest of my life with. **Tereza** has been a rock in my corner and now she's an amazing mom. I get plenty of joy from sharing insights into what helped me succeed in business. However, what brings me more joy is the beauty of parenthood and teaching my kids **Nico** and **Love Lolli** the same life lessons my parents taught me and more.

Aside from the support I've received from family, a big thank you goes out to the team that helped put this book together: My publishing company **Diversion Books** for seeing the vision I had for it and giving me the opportunity to get it into the public's hands and my co-author and friend, **Benjamin Platt. Ben**'s work on this project required him to be able to write in my voice and decipher the points I tried to convey through our long sessions together, and he did a great job at it. **Ben** worked as Rapid Realty's Communications Director for several years prior to taking on this assignment, and he really worked tirelessly to get this done.

I also want to give a special shout-out to **Joseph Dobrian** for his work early on in the process of putting this book together and getting some of the research and fact-checking done. I'm grateful for his contribution to this project and the unique perspective he brought to it.

To my core team members—both past and present—I thank you for your commitment to excellence and the stamina you continue to show day in and day out, which keeps the momentum going. I couldn't ask for a better partner than **Carlos Angelucci— My Woz** (see Part 1) and I can't speak highly enough of the job that **Marina Richards** has done over the years, carrying the heavy load of the management of administrative tasks—a list that has grown year after year. Thank you for your tremendous service and continued support.

Throughout the 20+ years I've run and operated my real estate business, there's been so much great talent that has contributed to the growth and success of our brands. From our award-winning technology to our unique marketing concepts, we've always had a solid team to depend on. Special thanks to **Dustin Buss, Mike Salvaggio,** and **Rusty Pancrazio** for always keeping us at the forefront of what's happening in the world of tech. Also, thank you **Gabriel Chapman** for your great title suggestion and for the

photography, videography, and media relations work you've done over the years.

To my Rapid Realty family: I want to thank all the franchisees, the top-producing agents, and all the tattoo brand ambassadors. I also want to give special acknowledgment to my senior franchisees who stuck with me and played a role in our growth. I want to thank our Franchise Expansion team— **Raymond "Ricco" Ruiz** and **Rodney Bonds**. **Ricco** and **Rodney** are leading the charge in expanding the Rapid brand into new markets, and their efforts are felt companywide. I also want to mention **Yeidy** and **Katherine Angelucci, Carlos**'s sisters, who are senior members of the franchisee family and have been with me since before we became a franchisor. They're the ones who brought their little brother into the business. I'd like to recognize all the military veterans serving our great country and risking their lives to keep us a free nation. One such veteran is my friend and top multi-unit franchisee **Adrian Cardona**, who has been a part of the Rapid family since we had just one office. The loyalty and devotion to the brand shown by **Adrian, Ricco, Rodney, the Angelucci family, and the rest of our senior franchisees and senior agents are unique in the real estate brokerage industry.**

My good friend **Charlie Brown** who passed away, **Nick Roussopoulos aka Nicky Brooklyn,** and **Jimmy Perez**—All of you hold a special place in my heart for your friendship and support.

I must thank my hard working public relations teams, **Frank Cipolla, Rich Lorenzen, Adam Weiss, Matthew Sheldon,** and **Linda Alexander,** as well as other PR people I've used throughout the years, and my good friend **Judy Sahagian**, who is a networking queen and has introduced me to many great contacts throughout our friendship. The exposure I've received from my PR team has helped get me the brand recognition that is necessary to become a household name in my industry.

I also have to acknowledge some of the press and media members I've met throughout this journey. I've always felt we were treated fairly by the press, and I've had the pleasure of getting to

know talented people like **Amir Korangy** (*The Real Deal*), **Vicki and Josh Schneps** (**Schneps Communications**), **Emily Smith** (**CBS**), **Teke Wiggin** (*Inman News*) and plenty of other journalists who have worked on stories about us.

Thank you to all of our social media followers and fans. I'm a pretty transparent guy, so be sure to follow me online to see what's going on in my world every day.

As mentioned in this book, you must have a good legal team behind you, looking after you and protecting you along the way. I've learned that you don't go to a Chinese restaurant and order pizza, so I've always worked with attorneys that are specialists in specific areas of law. I've received so much guidance throughout my career, and some of the people who provided that legal counsel are: **Phil Lavender, Richard Rosen, Michael Einbinder, Harold Kestenbaum, Peter Fields, Al Fazio, Ira Meyerowitz, Paul Petigrow, David Mollon, Peter Guadagnino** and others.

Throughout the book I also talk about real estate investing and financing. Over the years I've worked with many people in the world of real estate finance, but only a few stand out. I'd like to shout out **Jay Steinberg** and **Alex Freund** for coming through for me many times. I'd also like to give a special thank-you to **Wolf Landau** for his help in the early part of my real estate investing career. I can't mention finance without thanking **Jason Ozone** for all the support and structure he provided to our organization from its inception.

To my extended family, I thank you for your assistance, from my brother **Guido Pasquel** and his wife **Aileen** and my niece **Bianca,** to my cousin **Victor Lolli** and his wife **Judy**. Thank you to Judy's mother **Mildred Digiglio** for providing so much critical mentorship early on in my real estate career. When I first started she was the only person I called almost every day to ask questions on how to get deals done. Her advice and words of encouragement kept my spirits alive, and I'm forever grateful for it.

To my **Uncle Pancho, my Aunt Rosa, my grandmother Jesus, and my cousins Erika, Pancholin, and Jenny in Ecuador,**

thank you for your long-distance support and for being some of my biggest cheerleaders. I have always felt your sincere love and the prayers that you say for me.

I will never forget to thank my two main guys who run my construction jobs, who were there for me when I was just learning how to run a job site and have been working with me ever since. **Julio Alonzo and Sebastian** will always be more than just workers; they are my family, and I thank them for their role in my success. I also must mention **Ralph Succar**, a good friend and contractor who worked on projects with me including my home, **The Lolli Mansion**; and his nephew **George Makrinos**, who helped design the home and all of Rapid Realty's offices.

I also want to say thanks to **Richard Levine of New York Real Estate Institute** for providing people with a place to learn different facets of the real estate industry. It's facilities like his that allow people to get into this great business and start a new career.

Finally, I would never end this without mentioning the appreciation I have for what **Jehovah God** has provided me. I remain thankful for my opportunities, and I feel blessed to have had them.

ANTHONY LOLLI rose from humble beginnings to become a successful real estate investor, developer, entrepreneur, philanthropist, and author. A lifelong resident of Brooklyn, NY, Anthony got his real estate license at nineteen, and quickly became one of the top agents in the borough. At twenty-one, he bought his first investment property and turned the first floor into the home of his own brokerage firm, Rapid Realty NYC.

Under Anthony's watchful eye, Rapid Realty has grown into a national franchise sensation, and his real estate portfolio has expanded to include numerous buildings throughout New York City and beyond.

His dynamic and innovative leadership have garnered recognition both locally and on the international stage. He has received honors from the New York Urban League, International Business Awards, the Golden Bridge Awards, the Franchise Business Review, and the Inc. 5000, among others.

Anthony is a regular speaker at colleges, high schools, and business forums and he's a frequent guest on nationally broadcast television and radio programs, on networks including FOX Business, CNBC, and CNN, as well as local/regional programing. He is also an unabashed social media addict.

Stay in touch with Anthony

Send him your questions, and keep up with all the latest **Heart of the Deal** developments via:

f @AnthonyLolli

Instagram @AnthonyLolli

Twitter @Anthony_Lolli

in @AnthonyLolli

Snapchat @AnthonyLolli

AnthonyLolli.com
TheHeartOfTheDeal.com
LolliBrands.com